Full-Time RVing With Kids

An Insider's Guide To Life On The Road

By:

Bryanna Royal

Proofreading and editing by: Lynn Jurvis

Cover design by: Megan Jurvis Design

ISBN: 9798717887434

To Craig -

Thank you for supporting my ideas and passions.
This book wouldn't have been possible without you!

Live Q & A Session

If you are interested in one of our live question and answer sessions on full-time RVing with kids, you can learn more here:

www.crazyfamilyadventure.com/CFAQandA

(There is also a free gift: Our 15 Favorite RV Spots Guide!)

Table Of Contents

Praise for Full-Time RVing With Kids

Full-time Rving With Kids is a must-read for anyone thinking of jumping into full-time family travel. Bryanna Royal gives an incredibly detailed vision of what it is like to be a full-time rv family through the highs and lows of this lifestyle. No question is left unanswered! This is a resource I will be recommending to all the full-time family dreamers out there.

Nicole Schroeder, Fulltime Families

Full-Time RVing With Kids - An Insider's Guide To Life On The Road, is a must read for every family planning to hit the road. This book is a wealth of information and Bryanna delivers her full-time wisdom in an entertaining fashion. After reading this book, you will feel completely prepared to hit the road and prepare your family for an amazing Crazy Family Adventure of your own.

Marissa Moss, Less Junk More Journey

When I started RVing with a four-month-old, I had to toss the seat cushion under the table to fit the car seat at the dinette. Needless to say, I had NO IDEA how to add kids to our RV adventures. Bryanna has always been my go-to expert for any questions about RVing with kids because no doubt she's encountered every scenario under the sun while traveling. In her new book, she will prepare any parent (and any age kids!) for what life is really like full-timing as a family. A must-read for all parents before hitting the road with their kids.

Alyssa Padgett, Author of A Beginner's Guide To Living In An RV

When we rented our first RV, we turned to Crazy Family Adventure for guidance; and then when our family *bought* our first RV....we scoured their website once again. For years, Bryanna and Craig have been our go-to resource for so many things, the least of which is honest, real, no-nonsense advice on how to RV with kids. I am so thrilled about this book (I've already read it cover-to-cover several times) and the contents are invaluable. I can't recommend this book more!

Lesli Peterson, 365 Atlanta Traveler

Full-Time RVing With Kids An Insider's Guide To Life On The Road is the fast track to RVing with your family. This guide **will give you the tools and the confidence you need** as a RVing family. Bryanna's knowledge in explaining the lifestyle will help your family to be successful and have an amazing experience.

Jill Denkins, Family RV Caravans

If you are curious as to all the logistics of living with a family on the road, this is the book for you. So often the best way to learn is by hearing the stories of others, and Bryanna does an excellent job of not only crafting in her personal stories and experience, but also that of other full-time traveling friends she's met along the way!

She covers it all in this thorough book that covers the biggies you need to address before getting on the road, but also all those tiny little details that tend to bog us down, especially when it's unknown. Curious what appliances are best to splurge on, what apps you need to navigate, or exactly how you just handle privacy and daily living in an RV? She covers it.

Real-life, down to earth and practical, I've had the pleasure of knowing the Royals in person and recognizing they truly are an open book on sharing authentically and honestly how they have learned to truly thrive on the road.

Ashley Logsdon, Family Coach, Mama Says Namaste

Really wish an amazing resource like this would've been available when we first launched into full-time traveling. Authentic and full of great useful information, telling it like it is. A must for anyone dreaming, planning or starting RV traveling with their kids.

Shirly and Erez Weinstein, Zula Life

If you are planning to RV with your family full time. Bryanna is your GO TO resource to keep you sane while enjoying all the benefits of traveling full-time with your family. Bryanna is an amazing woman and mom and has helped our family go full time with such grace, ease and flow with her practical and down to earth tips. That make RV'ing fun and doable while running 2 businesses at the same time. This is a must read for anyone looking for a comprehensive approach to life on the road with kids!

Jenn Edden, Sugar Addiction Expert and Founder, The Sugar Freedom Method

The insight provided by Bryanna helped us to realize we could make our dream a reality. With both obvious and unexpected topics, we enjoyed reading, learning and preparing for our own adventures!

Jared and Summer Kunkel, Wandering_Kunks

Introduction

I am guessing you are reading this because you have come across the idea of full-time RV travel with your family. You've seen or heard about families doing this and you want in! But how are you going to get from here to there?

When you first realize you want to travel full time in an RV with your family, it can be very overwhelming. What about school? What RV will we get? How will we make money? Is it safe? Will my kids be OK?

We get it! We felt all the same things and had the exact same questions.

You are in the right place. Throughout this book I will share the ins and outs of full-time RV travel. This book was written to help you go from dreaming about this lifestyle to making it a reality.

I want to show you the good things, the confusing things, the scary things and the amazing things about this lifestyle! I'll honestly share my and my family's real thoughts and feelings about this whole process.

And I'll give you the real story behind the Instagram posts and the YouTube videos!

My husband, Craig, and I made the decision over 7 years ago to sell our suburbia dream house and most of the things in it, and move our 4 kids (Carson, Melia, Cannon and Knox) and our 2 dogs (Indy and Odin) into an RV to travel full-time.

Throughout those 7 years we have transitioned to being full-time entrepreneurs, lived in 5 different RVs and traveled all over the US and into Canada and Mexico.

There have been so many amazing and frustrating moments. There have been tears and joy and everything in between. I am excited to help you prepare for life on the road.

In chapter 1 I will get more into how we became a full-time RVing family. Next up we dive into 14 questions to ask yourself before becoming a full-time RVing family. (Question #1 is my favorite and the most important thing to ask yourself)

I will talk about how much this lifestyle can cost, how to make money on the road and the challenges of working in an RV with kids.

I'll cover how to pick a rig and share tips we have after being in 5 different rigs over the years. There will be ideas on how to downsize from your house to your RV and things you need to get ready for this lifestyle. Also, information on health Insurance, getting mail, apps to download and more.

Then I'll discuss how to handle different things once you're actually on the road. Things like making friends, having intimate time in the RV, holidays on the road, doctor and dentist visits and what to do when things go wrong. I will also share tips on having pets on the road, keeping your life simplified, different travel styles and planning your travels.

I will share my insights after being on the road for 1, 2 and 3 years. Then to wrap it up, I'll touch on the #1 thing that stops people from hitting the road with their family!

I know that seems like a lot! But, I wanted to do my best to anticipate and answer as many of your questions as I could while also giving you our real-life examples, experiences, thoughts and feelings accrued through 7 years of full-time RV travel with kids.

Ready?! Let's do this!!

Chapter 1

How We Became A Full-Time RVing Family

Being a full-time RV family was not something Craig or I ever thought we would be doing. So how did we get here? I'll start from the beginning.

Craig and I started dating when we were just 15, before we could even drive! We have been together ever since. Yup, high school sweethearts. While dating, we went on a few trips like your typical vacations to Mexico (Cancun 7 times – we really liked it there!) and snowmobiling up north. We were not big adventure travelers and liked going back to the same place. Because it was familiar we could get right into vacation mode of sitting on the beach watching the waves. And no RVing or camping . . . ever . . .

Both Craig and I were lucky enough to get great jobs right out of college (this was before the crash of 2008). Craig has a computer science degree, and I have a business degree in Marketing and Management Information Systems.

We both worked for 4 years building up our savings and getting ready for starting a family. Before we were even married, we knew I would stay home when we had kids, so we financially prepared for that.

After marrying, we built a house, sold a house, and then built our dream house (we had a lot of fun with the building process!) Seriously, this was the house we thought we would have grandkids visit us in.

After being married for just over 4 years, we welcomed our first son, Carson. A few years later we had girl/boy twins, Melia and Cannon (totally unexpected as twins don't run in our family and we weren't doing fertility treatments). Got pregnant again when the twins were a year old, had a miscarriage (it was never a viable pregnancy), then got pregnant a few months later with our 4th, Knox. All of this happened in less than 5 years. Whoa!

By the time we had 4 kids, we realized giving them all the attention they needed or we wanted to give them, was going to be a challenge, so we knew our family was complete.

We also had 2 dogs (labrador retrievers - Indy and Odin). They were our first fur babies!

So we had the American Dream. The perfect house in an amazing neighborhood, Craig had a great job. We had 4 kids and 2 dogs. Perfect, right?

But, it started to feel suffocating. We had accumulated so many toys and things to fill our house. We went almost every weekend to Target or Home Depot to buy things we thought we needed and things we did need to maintain our house.

Craig spent hours maintaining the yard and our pool. I spent hours trying to keep the house somewhat clean. Life was so busy, it was hard to find time for anything but keeping the kids fed and the house clean and maintained.

Over the years we discussed schooling and decided we were going to homeschool the kids. My parents are retired school teachers and were the ones who actually recommended we look into homeschooling. We researched a bunch of options and came across Radical Unschooling. It seemed like such an amazing fit and felt like the perfect transition from Attachment Parenting.

We researched Radical Unschooling, read books, joined Facebook groups, and decided we would give it a try. Knowing we were doing this really opened the door for other opportunities. We were no longer stuck to a school schedule. The year was ours.

We researched other things that we could do. We discovered families traveling around the world full-time with 4 kids. Wait, what?! People do this? At that time, it seemed too far-fetched to take our life and go in that direction.

Instead, we talked to my sister and her family about selling our houses and buying a duplex together so we could save money and travel on vacation days. But let's be serious, there isn't much traveling you can do when your husband only gets off for 4 weeks a year. And then there is the time over Christmas you want to take off to enjoy the holidays. Plus, we had pets we didn't want to leave behind.

That's when we discovered the idea of RV travel. Honestly, I don't remember how we came to it. But there it was, the option of traveling in an RV. We were still thinking we'd buy a duplex and then travel whenever we could.

We were excited about this! We bought a 29 foot Class C RV and figured we would give it a try. During this time, we had also put our house up for sale. We were ready for a change. We just didn't know how all the pieces were going to fit yet.

Putting the house up for sale was not easy. As I said, it was our dream home. Seriously, down to every last detail. We had designed it, painted it, built the deck, finished the basement. It was ours.

There were lots of tears and uncertainty. But there was excitement and, also, a fear we'd regret it if we didn't proceed. We forged ahead knowing we could always build another house if we wanted to.

We took our first long RV road trip down to northern Florida in January. I called my sister about 5 days in and said, "Hey, what do you guys think about selling our houses, each buying bigger RVs, and becoming full-time RV families?!"

They were on board! So, we laid out our plans. Well, kind of. Both of our husbands had jobs which we felt they still needed to keep at that time.

But since we had heard of other people doing it, we knew there were possibilities for jobs that allowed you to become nomadic.

We came home, kept downsizing and selling things, and searched high and low for an RV. Then we got an offer on the house. It just got real! More tears, more uncertainty, but we kept moving ahead, knowing we were ready for something more.

We signed the papers selling the house without having the RV. Crunch time! We finally found one on-line, negotiated a deal, and Craig flew down to Miami to pick it up and drive it all the way back to Wisconsin. Mind you, he'd never driven a huge Class A motorhome before.

He got home safely, and then the remodel began. We had just over a month from when he got home to clear out the house, and remodel the RV, so we all had somewhere to sleep. That month was a total blur!

We found a near-by RV park where we could stay from May until October, and my sister and her family would be in a spot next to us! Our husbands would continue to go into work Monday thru Friday, and we would figure out our next step from there.

The day came when it was time to leave the house and start the RV lifestyle. Man, that was hard. We stood in the kitchen and bawled our eyes out, feeling like we couldn't physically walk away.

This was our dream house. What the heck were we doing?! But we had come this far, and like we said, wanted no regrets, no what-ifs.

So we did it. We walked out, turned over the keys, and started the next chapter in our life. That was almost 7 years ago!

Throughout the book I will share more about our journey and what we have been doing over the last 7 years. I will share the ups and downs and the how-tos. And, also, our viewpoints on this lifestyle, entrepreneurship, schooling, and so much more!

I want to start with sharing 14 questions to ask yourself before you decide to hit the road full time with your family. Buckle up and let's do this!!

Chapter 2

14 Things To Ask Yourself Before Deciding To Go Full-Time With Your Family

You see all the cool social media posts from traveling families, and you think YES, we can do that! We get it. We felt the same way before we decided to go full-time. Then we launched and realized there were a few things it would have been nice to know. So here you go. Fourteen questions to ask yourself BEFORE you decide to sell it all and hit the road 24/7 with your kids.

After that we will share the number one thing we think you need to know before you hit the road and our seven favorite things about full-time travel and the seven things we find challenging about full-time travel. Let's do this!

Do you like your family?

You may have chuckled with this one. But there is a reason this is the first question. When you travel full-time, you are with your family 24/7.

Seriously.

Grandma isn't down the street, or the kids aren't going to school five days a week.

It is you and them.

All.

The.

Time.

Yes, you may make friends at campgrounds or find friends you travel with, which will break up some of that time, but there aren't always other kids at campgrounds, and usually, you don't travel 100% of the time with another family.

Don't get me wrong; this is one thing I also LOVE about full-time family travel. But it isn't always easy and is different than the busy life we had when we were living in our house.

When on the road, there can be a lot of downtime for you and your family. It can lead to great bonding, playing, and just hanging out as a family, but can also be overwhelming.

It took some getting used to, and it was fantastic having family visit and travel with us sometimes. It was nice for us and our kids to meet people at the campgrounds and make friends which helped break up that 24/7 family time, too.

Is Your Body Ready For It?

This one caught us by surprise. We were in pretty good shape before we left, but this life is physical, especially if you move often. Every time you move, there is packing up, un-hooking, and getting things ready to go. That takes a lot out of you.

When you are visiting places, you usually are out exploring, walking around cities, hiking, swimming, etc. Again, it can be exhausting. But so much fun, too!!!

Of course, you could decide to take a slower approach to how often you travel and what you do at locations. But if you are like us and want to get out and see and do a lot and move every week or two, be ready for it!

Are You A Planner?

Do you like planning? You can choose to travel less and stay in places for longer, meaning less planning. But you still need to figure out where you will stay and what you will do when you are there.

If you plan to travel a lot (every couple of weeks or even more often), it takes a lot of time to find places to stay, things to do, and all the logistics that go along with that.

I have a love/hate relationship with this part. It takes time, and as anyone who works and has a family knows, time is limited! But it is also so rewarding to learn about new locations and to put together a fantastic trip!

Be aware that planning can take hours each week or even a few days to a week to get your whole year planned out and scheduled. We have scheduled about a month ahead of time and have tried to plan further out. But over the years, we have learned that we prefer not to plan too far out, and just go with the flow and figure it out week by week or sometimes day by day.

If there is a certain place or campground we want to stay at we may make a reservation far in advance and just know we can cancel it. And will usually have to pay a fee if we do cancel.

Are You Ready To Not Be On Vacation?

This was a tough one! When you first start, we recommend adding a few extra thousand dollars to your budget as you work through this. The first place you go, you will want to do and see everything and act as if you are on vacation. The expenses quickly add up, and you start to realize, "Wait a second, we can't do this every place we go, or else we will be broke!"

We always Google "FREE things to do in..." (the locations we are going to). There are a lot of free things to do around the country. We have also really gotten into hiking, which is excellent since it is free!

Are You Prepared To Be Homesick?

It may not be homesick like a kid can be for their family when they leave to go to camp or college for the first time - or maybe it can be. But it's also just missing the familiarity of being in a city that you know. Where you have your favorite coffee shop, and you know where everything is in the grocery store. Or even that when you go to the store you always run into people that you know. Being on the road in new and unfamiliar places all the time is very different from this.

Are You Ready To Question and Doubt Yourself?

We have continuously questioned and sometimes doubted our decision to live our life this way. But we always come back to knowing we could never go back to our old life, and we are having so much darn fun that we don't want to stop! It doesn't mean that the doubt doesn't sneak in . . .

I think that has to do with living an unconventional lifestyle. I also think it is just life in general. If you are someone who questions and analyzes things, that does not go away when you start this life.

Are You OK Being the Oddball?

You will be that family. The one your in-laws or high school classmates talk about as being the crazy people that sold their house to hit the road. Don't worry. They are all probably a little bit jealous, or they may genuinely think you are crazy, and that is OK. To each his own. Just be prepared for it to happen. Then smile and wave as you head out on another fantastic adventure!

Are You Ready To Be Changed Forever?

Are you ready to expand your comfort zone, thought process, and beliefs further than you ever thought possible?! Are you prepared to know what freedom feels like? Once you go down this road, it will forever change you.

This way of life has ruined us for a normal life – in a good way! But we also feel if we ever hit a time to be ready to settle down again, we will be happy in the decision (at least for a while) since we will make it with all the experiences and knowledge we have gained from traveling.

They will be OUR decisions, not decisions based on the masses or what everyone else is doing. But a decision based on what we know is the right direction to go with our family. Or at least what we want the next step to be. Each step leads us down the path that works for us.

Ready To Awaken Your Wanderlust Bug?

Once you know all the amazing things out in the world and experience them at a slow and leisurely pace, you won't want to stop exploring! We traveled a little bit growing up and before kids, but it wasn't a strong focus in our life. Now I couldn't imagine going months without exploring somewhere new.

Can You Leave Simple Behind?

Yes, our life is simplified when it comes to things. But it isn't simple in the sense that we can't go home on a Friday night to a house that we know and just relax for the weekend. We are always thinking a few steps ahead of where we want to go next and what we want to do. We love that part of our life, but it takes away the simplicity of just knowing what your days and weeks are going to look like.

Are You Able To Leave The Structure You Are Used To?

When your time becomes "Your Time", the structure goes out the window. No boss to tell you when to be somewhere. No school is telling you when to drop off and pick your kids up. It is all in your control. Amazing and scary! We are still figuring this one out!

Can You Grocery Shop In An Unfamiliar Place?

I had to add this one. This is no joke. As a Mom trying to feed our family as healthy and cheaply as possible, this is a definite challenge . . .

Can You Be Mr. Or Mrs. Fix-It?

Whether you have an RV or travel via planes, trains, or automobiles, things break. If you hired someone to fix everything that breaks or goes wrong while traveling, you would blow your budget pretty quickly.

If you're brave enough to fix things on your own, even if you have no idea how (hello, Google and YouTube!), then you have a fighting chance to keep traveling for a while.

Are You Ready to Have the Most Amazing Adventure of Your Life With Your Family by Your Side?

Are you? Hopefully, yes!! Can you deal with 1 – 13 so you can go on this amazing adventure? That's why we do this, and that's why we love it! This roller coaster ride of emotions, stress and comfort zone stretching is one wild ride, but it is worth it. We live our lives by our terms, and we are so glad that we went for it.

How did you do? Are you ready?! In all honesty, we say even if all of these questions scared you or made you think twice, just go for it! We did not have all the answers before we started, and if we waited until we did, we never would have left. We hope this list helps people prepare mentally for traveling full-time as a family and to realize that it takes a little (OK, maybe a lot) of crazy to live this way, but it is worth it and doable!

Making The Decision To Hit The Road

OK, you made it past the 14 questions - and you still want to travel full-time with your kids - AWESOME! The next step is looking at all the components that go into making this lifestyle change. **We are going to start with what we consider the most important: Know your WHY.**

Why are you deciding to hit the road as a family?

- Are you looking to save money for something in the future?
- Are you looking to get out and travel?
- Are you looking to spend more time together as a family?
- Are you bored with your current life and want to try something else?
- Do you want to start your own business?
- Do you crave freedom?

Or maybe there is a whole other reason why you want to do this. Whatever your why is, own it! There may be hard, really hard, times as you transition to this new lifestyle. You will question, doubt, cry, laugh, get excited, get scared, be confused - all within an hour as you prepare to move into this lifestyle.

But, if you know your WHY, it will keep moving you forward to reach your goal of hitting the road. You may have a whole life currently set up with a beautiful house, a great job, great friends. That will continuously pull at you! For this reason, really focus on your WHY so you can keep yourself moving forward. Or else, before you know it, five years will have gone by, and you won't have made your dreams a reality.

The other important part of knowing your why is that it can determine many of your choices in this lifestyle. If your goal is to save money, then you probably won't be doing this to travel, because traveling costs lots of money from gas to campgrounds, to paying for activities.

In our case, we wanted to be able to try out new restaurants at new locations, do fun activities with the kids, and stay at excellent campgrounds on the beach sometimes. There will be more about ways to do this for less throughout the book. BUT, if travel is a big part of your why, it will be hard to save money - trust us on this one.

It is also essential at this point to talk to your kids - even if they are young - to ask what their thoughts are on this adventure. What is their WHY? Maybe it is to hang out more with Mom and Dad, and that is great. Or perhaps they have plans, too, and are excited to meet new friends, visit new places, or have a slower life pace (no more soccer practice).

Our WHY is Family, Freedom, Travel. We have tried to focus on this with all of the decisions we have made throughout the last 7 years.

Next up we share the seven things we love about full-time family travel and what has kept us on the road for 7 years!

Seven Things We Love About Full-Time Family Travel

(We had been on the road for over two years when we wrote this, and there had been ups and downs. It had been a wild ride!)

We enjoy so many things about this lifestyle, and we want to share our top seven things we love about full-time RVing!

Learning about all of the unique places there are in the US

Sure we (my husband and I) learned all about the US in school, but it is nothing compared to driving the country and seeing everything first hand.

The difference between the East Coast, Midwest, South, West, Mountains, desert, ocean, etc., is impressive. The feels, smells, and vibes of all of these different locations are so unique and fascinating.

The freedom

We literally can go and do anything we want to do. Okay, it isn't quite that cut and dry, but the reality is if we wanted to get up tomorrow and drive across the country, we could. If we wanted to stay in one location for six months, we could. If we don't like a place, we can leave.

It is a liberating feeling to know you are totally in control of your life and where you go next. It has been eye-opening and challenging to learn how to handle this. Both my husband and I are from the box of "normal." Meaning we came from a white picket fence background where we went to public school, went to college, and then got jobs. A lot of that life was predetermined for us – even if we didn't know that. We were following the masses. Now we sometimes feel like we are on an island and there is no one guiding us. . . it can be scary, but in the end, it is also amazing.

Family time

Full-time RVing allows us to be with our family 24/7. How many times do you talk to an older couple, and they mention how fast time goes? How your kids are grown and out of the house before you know it. We see that happening. But we also took that to heart and have designed our life where we are with our kids all of the time. We're trying to soak in as much of this time we have with them before they leave home to live their own lives.

This has been instrumental in deepening our family bond. When the kids have questions, they come to us. If they are upset, we are there to help them through it. When there is a challenge, we are here to help guide them. When they are excited about something, we are there to be excited right along with them. We are all so deeply entwined in each other's life. It is a fantastic thing.

Experiences

The experiences we have had as individuals and as a family throughout this full-time RVing journey are truly unbelievable. Hiking to mountain summits, swimming with dolphins, petting whales in Mexico, walking on a Glacier, seeing Yellowstone, exploring Canada, visiting Death Valley, the Utah National Parks, and more. It is all so unique and surreal. Had we not chosen full-time RVing, there is no way that we would have been able to experience all of these fantastic places together as a family.

There just would not have been enough time in the year or enough money to make it happen. By making full-time travel a focus of our life, we have experienced so many places and things. And we are choosing to share them as a family vs. as a retired couple. It is one of the best decisions we have made. Seeing these experiences through our kids' eyes is exceptional, and we are so happy to be a part of it.

Down time

Living life on the road means we have slow mornings, snuggle time, and a lot of time to just hang out. We aren't rushing from one activity to the next or having a packed schedule of things to do. Instead, we have a lot of downtime where we can relax together as a family. It can take us 2 to 3 hours to get up, eat breakfast, and get ready to head out the door in the morning.

It is nice to have the luxury to take that time in the morning and not have to be somewhere by 8 am. It gives everyone a chance to wake up slowly and enjoy snuggling in bed in the morning multiple days a week.

Interestingly, this can be an issue during the winter when it gets dark earlier. Suddenly, we're running out of daylight to do the things we'd planned.

Simplified living

Before living this lifestyle, we lived in a large house filled with things. Seriously filled. Living life this way has shown us how little we need to live a fulfilling life. I can honestly say there are only a handful of things that we miss from our house (a nice big bathtub, the trampoline in the backyard for the kids to burn energy, a stove for baking cookies - that is all I can think of).

Living a simplified life is so much, well, simpler. It is less to maintain, less to take care of, and less to worry about. It also makes us better understand the things we do want from a materialistic standpoint. Which then makes them mean more when we have them.

For example, I want a nice warm zip-up sweatshirt – I want a longer one with a zipper, which is important to me. These days, I'm not going to run to Target just to buy one. Instead, I look for a brand I want to support and – it has to feel right and look good because it is the only one I'll have.

The kids now realize that there are toys they have that they never played with – and when we talk about it, they get it. It makes them more thoughtful when they choose a new toy and to think about what toys they want to keep. When we go through everything to re-simplify – which we do at least once a month, they have an easier time choosing what to keep and what to get rid of.

Simplified living has helped us better understand ourselves and given us the ability to think through and understand our decisions when making a purchase, which opens up room in our life for more experiences and time together as a family.

We can do anything we set our mind to

Making this crazy leap to break away from the rat race and live life on our terms has taught us we can do anything we want to do. It isn't always an easy path, but it is possible. We just have to put our heads together, decide what we want, and then make it happen. We now know we can do that, because we've done it. And as everyone knows, once you have done it once, it is easier to do it again.

Full-time family travel isn't always rainbows and sunshine. But overall, the challenges we face have been worth it for all the things we love about it. This process has been more eye-opening to us as individuals and a family than we were expecting.

Full-time RVing isn't just about traveling to new places. It's about so much more. It's about pushing our comfort zones, taking control of our life and living with a purpose!

There you have it. The seven things that we love about life on the road. Now we will share the seven things we find challenging about life on the road!

Seven Things We Find Challenging About Full-Time Family Travel

Of course, along with all of the great things about it there are challenges to this lifestyle. We wanted to be sure to share those too! Here are 7 (almost 8) things we find challenging about full-time RVing with kids.

Leaving family and friends

This is one thing that doesn't go away, but you get used to it the longer you are on the road.

We knew this would be an issue when we talked about hitting the road, we cried about it, and we questioned it. The hardest thing about life on the road is leaving family and friends back home, and then leaving friends made while on the road when we move on. Since we have been on the road my Grandpa and my Grandma passed away. In both cases, I was not back home when this happened. If we were still living in our house, I would have been there for every part of it. That was a hard thing to deal with.

There is guilt around not being there to see them the weeks or days leading up to their passing and not having the chance to say that last goodbye. I know that is life, and that is how it is for a lot of people. But in our old life, it wasn't like that. We were there for everything.

Leaving to go on the road brings on many tears and sad faces. We question ourselves as we watch the tears stream down our kids' faces when they have to say goodbye to their cousins and family. And it's so sad to leave behind amazing friends that your kids have known since they were born.

The truth is, it sucks!! We have a fantastic family and group of friends back home. And I was guilty of not fully appreciating them until we hit the road, and couldn't see them anymore.

So, YES, we question this aspect of traveling more than anything else! But we love our new life and are enjoying our adventures, and we realize we couldn't be having all of these wonderful experiences or bonding as a family the way we are if we'd stayed in our house.

We are lucky that my sister and her family travel, too. They actually got on the road the same day we did. A few years later my parents sold their house and hit the road full-time. We spend a good amount of time throughout the year traveling together which is fun!

And we keep posting away on social media to show all of our friends in Wisconsin how nice and warm and sunny the beach is hoping it will convince them to travel south this winter to see us!!

I know this will always be one of the hardest parts of traveling, and we hope all of our family and friends understand, and see that we did not make this decision lightly. We keep hoping ALL of them will join us on the road! Now that would be an EPIC caravan!!

We have gotten more used to the goodbyes over the years. Maybe it's because we know how much fun it is when we see each other again. Or maybe because when we see friends and family, we cherish the time we have together more!

Another aspect I wasn't expecting was a fear of what our future will look like when our kids are grown up. Will they end up living worldwide and never have a home base where we all celebrate holidays together? Will they live a constant life of wanderlust?

Both Craig and I grew up in a typical lifestyle, going to school, doing sports/activities, having lots of family and friends around. So we're not sure about the future we are building for our kids living our lives this way. We are excited, yet nervous about this. But we also know we will follow our kids wherever they go - we have warned them about this!

Not having your own yard or kids' bedrooms to mess up or decorate

When we started full-time RVing and moved into our first location at Jellystone Park. When we started full-time RVing, I noticed this one almost immediately. We had lived in a house with a half-acre fenced-in backyard, and we let the kids paint on the fence or play with shaving cream on the deck. We also had a large sandbox, a pool, a trampoline, and a swing set. We were planning on adding in a mud pit and playhouse.

The kids had lots of room to run and lots of freedom to do what they wanted. When you move into an RV park, suddenly, you are living on someone else's property . . . and they may not want you painting all over their picnic table or even coloring with chalk on their cement.

It was an adjustment. It has forced us to change our parenting style in a way we didn't want to but needed to in order to live this lifestyle. We still try to find opportunities to let the kids play the way they used to, but it takes a lot more planning now.

As for the bedrooms, each of the kids had their own bunk bed, so this area became their space. They picked the color they wanted the walls painted and also put stickers up. This has helped give them their space, but they don't have much room for things like completed Lego creations or a doll bed.

Not having a bedroom means everything always needs to be cleaned up and put away, since there just isn't room to leave things out. With a bedroom or basement, you could shut the door and forget about it. Not so much when you are living in such a small space.

We have chosen to give these things up to live this lifestyle. Our kids did not choose this, yet we ask them often if they want to keep traveling, and almost 100% of the time, the answer is yes. But it doesn't mean they don't miss these things because they do. However, they have done a great job moving on and letting go.

Moving days

Moving Days are the days Craig and I always question what we are doing . . . until we get where we're going and realize how cool and exciting it is to get out and explore a new place! Over the years, we have gotten better at moving days and hope when we downsize we can simplify it even more.

Having a rig with four slide-outs and beds that have to be put away and then set back up each time we move adds to the frustration. Plus having to move car seats in and out of the rig. Then there is the actual driving . . .

Driving a rig that is almost 40′ long plus towing the car is no stroll in the park. I don't drive it, but I ride in it, and I am aware of how big we are, and it is stressful! I swear we are going to hit mirrors with every semi we drive past.

Then in the back, the kids are yelling for food, needing to use the bathroom, and generally whining about everything. Well, everyone with kids gets the ups and downs of a road trip!

Missing the familiar

There is comfort in the familiar. We gave most of that up living a life of full-time family travel. Yes, the rig is familiar, which is perfect as our home base and why we like this style of traveling vs. hotels, house swapping, or AirBnB's. However, each time we get to a new location, we have to learn where we are and what the layout is for the city.

Driving in the car with kids used to be my downtime since I knew where I was going. I didn't have to concentrate on directions. Not the case when you are in a new location. Thank goodness for Google Maps. Visiting all these new places is part of why we do this, but it isn't always easy!

Being back in Wisconsin reminds us of the familiar and how good it feels. It won't stop us from wanting to hit the road again. But now we enjoy the familiarity of being home and appreciate it more!

Grocery stores

Craig laughs, and I know I have mentioned it before, but man, this is so true!! You know how you have a favorite grocery store. Maybe the prices are right, the produce is excellent, whatever it may be. Boy, do I miss that. Now I am going to a new grocery store multiple times a month, and it is like starting your first day at a new school.

I don't know where anything is, and the stores don't have my brands. Things cost way more than I am used to paying. Trying to feed a family and stay on a budget is not easy when you are in an unfamiliar grocery store. The cool part is they usually have a local specialty – like fresh-picked cherries or Huckleberries, so I try to take advantage of those.

When we went back to Wisconsin last time, I happened to run into my sister at our favorite grocery store, and we were both like, WOW, it is so cheap here! Did you see the price for avocados?? It was too funny.

Never ending wanderlust

We have awakened this never-ending wanderlust that we seriously didn't know we had. Having lived this lifestyle for a while now, I don't know if we could ever go back to a "normal" life.

Our eyes are open to this fantastic world, and we want to see more, touch more, smell more of it. And wow, we live in a big and beautiful world; there is so much more to see.

As I mentioned above, this does scare me a little bit because our kids will eventually grow up and go out on their own. Have we awakened this wanderlust in them so we will have to work hard to keep track of them when they leave?

We joke that either they will buy a house in a city and never travel, or they will end up sailing down the Amazon river and exploring even more and deeper than we ever have. Only time will tell!

Close neighbors

This is a tough one. We aren't perfect, and our kids aren't perfect. We yell, we cry, we laugh loudly, and we fight loudly. The kids wrestle - all the time. And our neighbors are 10 feet away. When the windows are open the noise travels quickly. This is hard with kids.

We feel embarrassed and worried that everyone can hear everything that goes on in our rig and that it isn't always pretty. We have to tell ourselves that when people stay in an RV park, they expect that. We also are as considerate as possible, but there are just times when the kids are going to break down and cry. A lot and loudly.

It took getting used to, but it is part of what we have to be okay with if we are going to travel the way we are. Yes, we could go boondock in places where no one else is around, and we may end up doing that. But for now, we aren't.

Almost 8. 1 Bathroom For 6 People

When we first started, I thought this would be on the list since we left a house with three full bathrooms and half bath. Actually, it's not that big of a deal.

Yes, there have been a few times we have had to take the boys outside (I mean to the bathroom at the campground) to pee or have to rush someone, so someone else doesn't poop on the floor! But for the most part, it hasn't been an issue.

And guess what that means? One toilet to clean, not 4!! That is a win in my book.

We were never under the impression that this lifestyle would turn our life into a perfect life that had no issues. So we are okay with these challenges and continue to work on making them less of a challenge. But hey, like with anything, things are never going to be perfect, and we focus on accepting that and enjoying all the fantastic things that full-time family travel brings to our family and us.

Alright, there you have it - the good, the bad and the uncertainty. I told you we would try to be as honest as possible. Also note we have been on the road almost 7 years so . . . that says a lot too.

Next up, we will break down how much it costs. We will share exact numbers along with our budget for a few months on the road, and more!

Chapter 3

How Much Does It Cost

How much does full-time RV travel with kids cost? This can be a hot topic for people! There are those who want to tell you how cheap it can be, and those who go on the road with money and are ready to spend. And everyone in between. The reality is it all depends on how you want to travel and spend your money.

For this first section, I will take you back to when we had been on the road for 2 years. Things have changed over the years. But this is still a good representation of what this lifestyle can cost. At that time, we were careful with our money. This was also when Craig quit his job, and we became full-time entrepreneurs. Now we tend to spend more . . . and don't have to watch every penny.

There are a lot of different full-time RV lifestyles. Are you looking at this lifestyle to save money, to go on an ultimate road trip moving every few days, or do you want to stay in RV parks for months at a time? These things do factor into how much full-time RV living costs.

We had not chosen this lifestyle to save money. For us, we always wanted to travel and travel a lot. We moved every few days or after 1-2 weeks.

That being said, when we first hit the road, we were spending a TON of money. Way more than the bills we had on our house!! It was crazy. We were like, wait a minute, how are we going to sustain this?! That winter, we went to a Thousand Trails campground and met up with many other full-time RVing families and talked to them about their budget.

WOW - they were all doing it for a lot less than we were! We continued to research and understand the different options outside of just private campgrounds. Things like Thousand Trails memberships, boondocking, weekly or monthly stays, and other different ways we could lower our campground expenses.

We also talked about how, if you're trying to stay on a lower budget, you can't go and do all the cool paid activities at each location you visit, instead, look for National/State Parks, National Recreation Sites, free museums and other things like that. Our favorite Google search became: Free Things To Do In....

Over time our budget ebbed and flowed, and we tried a lot of different things.

We will start by sharing our basic bills for full-time family travel. Next, we will show what our budget and spending was for 2 different months on the road.

Our Bills for Full Time Family Travel

RV payment: $533 a month

This was for a 15-year loan on a Class A Diesel Pusher Motorhome

Car payment: $320 a month

Insurance: $170 a month

RV, car, and our things – since we didn't have homeowner's insurance, we needed a policy on items inside the RV since the RV insurance does not cover that.

My cell phone: $55 a month: Through Straight Talk – with Verizon coverage – 10g data and unlimited talk and text. I had previously purchased a phone outright.

Craig's cell phone: $49 (he purchased a phone outright as well)

Internet: $70 a month

This is really low and one of the biggest challenges for families living on the road. The key is to keep an eye out for new unlimited plans that pop up. These have proven not to last very long, but you never know. In reality, you should expect to pay closer to $200 a month for internet. It all depends on your needs, though.

Kids stock: $50 a month

We invest $50 each month and rotate which kid gets it. No, $150 a year isn't much for each kid, but it is something.

Hulu: $12 a month

Life Insurance: $64 a month for Craig and me.

Thousand Trails Membership: $50 a month

We bought a used membership to the Thousand Trails system. This is basically a campground timeshare. The membership cost $3,000, which we paid upfront, but we have to pay $550 yearly. The membership allowed us to stay for free at any Thousand Trails campground. We can stay for 2 - 3 weeks at a time; then we had to go to another Thousand Trails campground. We could have camped all year for free if we always stayed at a Thousand Trails campground. We didn't do that, but this really helped offset higher-costing campgrounds we stayed at. I will explain more about these memberships later in the book.

Health Insurance: $178 a month

This was through the Marketplace. We got a subsidy from the state we were residents of – Wisconsin. Yes, this was low. But we didn't make much money, and had 6 people, so we got an outstanding subsidy. We were nervous about what was going to happen in the coming years . . . More on health insurance options in a future chapter.

This came to $1,561 a month for our bills.

Living Expenses for Full Time Family Travel

Next came living expenses. Things like food, gas, paying for our campsites, and spending money. These costs really varied and were part of what we tried to work on. That said, these numbers are not 100% accurate since they changed from month to month. But this is what we aimed for.

Groceries: $1000 – $1200 a month

We would have liked this to be more in the $800 range. But we also liked to buy organic and felt it was worth the extra money.

Gas for the car: $150 a month

To be honest, I had no idea how accurate this would be. And it all depended on the activities that we did in that month and how far we drove.

Campgrounds: Free to $2,100 a month

We wanted to aim for $600 a month. Yes, there was quite a difference between $0 and $2,100. We chose a couple of locations that year that were out of our budget range, but we splurged. If we were really trying, we wanted it to be around $600, which we did some months, but other months, we were way over.

Spending: $500 – $1000 a month

Again, it varied, and we were trying to keep it at $500 for a month. Spending money was what we spent on activities, going out to eat, and any other money we spent here or there.

Extras:

- RV Gas: $300 or more a month - It depended on where we were traveling.
- RV Maintenance and repairs: ?? Who knew! An oil change cost a couple hundred dollars, but how often we needed one depended on how far we had driven. And you never knew when something was going to need to be fixed with the RV. So it was tough to plan for. We basically figured our savings would just have to cover it.

Living expenses came out to $2500 – ? per month.

Adding that to the bills came to about $4200 a month.

Obviously, this did not include savings or retirement planning and also did not leave a lot of room for error. We had decided to change our lifestyle, so we could work less, and live more on the edge learning to be comfortable with the unknown.

Other families made a lot more money and spent a lot more money than us, and other families learned to live on less than us. So please don't think this is the only way this lifestyle works.

We also both had 401Ks from previous jobs. Should we still have been saving for retirement? Yes. Was that a priority? Not so much when we were kind of living our retirement already! But we did want to add in retirement planning again when possible.

No, we weren't actively adding to our savings. Would that make some people uncomfortable? Yes. Did it make us uncomfortable? Not really. We were living for the moment and putting our money into that.

Would we have liked to save? Yes, and were sure we would in the future.

Update: Now that our businesses have grown, we save money and add to our retirement.

Sample Budget For 1 Month

Our fiscal month ran from September 14th – October 13th. Our credit card cycle closed then, and what we spent that month would be due on November 11th. That gave us time to find more work/money if we needed to! We put as many of our expenses/bills as we could on our Chase Sapphire Preferred card. That way, we could accumulate points to be used for things like purchases on Amazon, hotel rooms (nice to get out of the RV sometimes), air flight, etc.

Our monthly budget goal was $4000 for everything. That was for a family of 6 plus 2 dogs living and traveling full-time in our RV. We never hit that $4000. . . it was always more.

Places we visited during this time:

- September 14th – September 25th - Yellowstone National Park (RV Park)
- September 25th – September 28th – Salt Lake City, Utah (State Park)
- September 28th – October 6th – Moab, Utah (RV Park)
- October 6th – October 12th – Goblin Valley State Park, Utah and Capitol Reef National Park, Utah (Boondocked – stayed for free on BLM land)
- October 12th – October 14th – Bryce Canyon National Park (RV Park)

What We Spent for 1 Month:

Business expenses: $672

Groceries: $1115.20 (I would have liked this to be $1000 – we were close!)

Gas for RV and Car: $402.54

We didn't travel that far during this time. Another month, our RV gas alone could end up being $300 if we went further. Gas for the car was normally $150 – $200 depending on what we did.

Campground Fees: $592

This included campgrounds plus our monthly Thousand Trails membership ($46.49).

This total included staying for free on BLM land for 6 nights. We also chose to stay at an RV park about 30 minutes from Bryce Canyon National Park and 90 minutes from Zion National Park (which we drove to twice) since the cost was that much less than staying at a place right by Zion.

At Yellowstone, we got a discount since our brother-in-law was working there.

(We had this budgeted at $600 – $800, but our goal was always to be less. The next month, we stayed at Thousand Trails resorts for 6 weeks straight so had no campground fees during that time – except for the monthly Thousand Trails bill.)

RV Repairs/Maintenance Car Repairs/Maintenance: $79.68

Car Oil Change & other routine maintenance (always liked when this cost was low for the month, but knew that wasn't the reality every month).

Medical/Pharmacy: $143.22

Luckily, it was just for one of our dogs that month.

Experiences: $72

This was for paid experiences We could sometimes get these for free if we blogged about them. Other times we paid. Then there were times we found free stuff in the area (one of the many reasons we loved hiking!). Plus, we had a yearly pass to all the National Parks – the best $80 we spent! That month was a lot about hiking and free activities. Utah was a great place for that!

One thing we paid for was the Arches Fiery Furnace Hike Permits. It was worth it!

Bills: $1561

These were the monthly bills as mentioned above.

Extra/Spending/Eating Out: $643.14

These were the extras like kid's toys, listing our RV, video rentals, Google Play purchases, parking, etc. It really varied each month. We wanted to keep this at $500 for the month, but that was really hard.

In Summary:

- Business expenses: $672
- Groceries: $1115.20
- Gas for car and RV: $402.54
- Campground Fees: $592
- RV Repairs/Maintenance Car Repairs/Maintenance: $79.68
- Medical/Pharmacy: $143.22
- Experiences: $72
- Bills: $1561
- Extra Spending: $643.14

Total: $4280.78

Over by $280.78 . . . we wanted to be at the $4000 mark each month.

Over budget – why I think this happened:

I did not calculate enough for business expenses (having to pay for the internet in Yellowstone didn't help). We overspent in the Extras category – made a note to avoid Target – we always spent way too much there. It was better to order what we needed via Amazon, where we knew how much our total was before we placed the order. Groceries were over by $115, which wasn't too bad.

Eating out, experiences and extra should have all equalled $500, not over $600. We didn't really budget for medical or car/RV repairs. Figured if we had to go into savings for those we would. That was one of the things we had to accept with this lifestyle.

From an income perspective, we were close to covering everything through work we did or work we had coming in. If we couldn't cover everything, we had to pull from savings and then work to put that back the next month (we didn't want to do this). We basically had the next month to get the money we needed, which I knew we could do! Another thing we had to accept and get comfortable with was the idea that we could make money if we hustled to find it, and did good work.

Summary of PLANNED expenses for the next month:

Business Expenses: $284.50

Food/Groceries: $1000

Gas for RV and Car: $450

Campground Fees: $50

We had already paid for where we were staying at the time and where we would be staying in southern Arizona. We were going to be doing some boondocking (camping somewhere free without any hook-ups), and then staying at a Thousand Trails – so $50 was the Thousand Trails Membership.

RV/Car Repair/Maintenance: ?

Who knew? Hopefully low.

Medical/Pharmacy: $200

Had a medical bill from a doctor's appointment and a dentist bill.

Spending (Including eating out, experiences, extra): $500

Bills: $1561

The total for the month would be: $4,045.50

For that next month, we planned to visit Zion National Park, Grand Canyon, I would be attending a travel blog conference, and then we would explore as much of Arizona as we could.

Here was our actual spending for that next month:

Places we visited during that time:

- October 14th – October 19th – Bryce Canyon National Park and Zion National Park in Utah (RV Park)
- October 19th – October 21st – Grand Canyon (Boondocked on BLM land in the National Forest)
- October 21st – October 22nd – Phoenix (stayed for free in a Casino parking lot)
- October 22nd – October 29th – Catalina State Park in Tucson, Arizona
- October 29th – November 1st – Phoenix (stayed for free in a

Casino parking lot)
- November 1st – November 14th – Verde Valley, Arizona at a Thousand Trails (We were members, so we stayed for free)

Spending for October 14th – November 14th

Business expenses: $588.19

Groceries: $926.21

Included groceries, beer and wine. We were under budget by $74!

Gas for RV and Car: $657.50

We did a lot of traveling that month . . . but we saw a lot of cool places, too!

Campground fees: $46.49

We stayed at many free places that month, and the campgrounds we stayed at had been paid for when we made the reservations the month before. The $46.49 was our Thousand Trails monthly membership fee. We also planned on staying at a lot of Thousand Trails, so we didn't have to pay to make reservations anywhere for the next month.

RV Repairs/Maintenance Car Repairs/Maintenance: $0

Always a good thing when it was $0!

Medical/Pharmacy: $100

Made payments on an old medical bill from back home.

Experiences: $44.37

That month was a lot about hiking and free activities in the National Parks. And most of the money went towards buying stickers at the parks or paying to get into a State Park.

Bills: $1561

These were the monthly bills we had to pay every month.

Extra Spending/Eating Out: $975.31

The RV park we were at was way too close to a Walmart, which meant many impulse buys. Plus, we finally had somewhere to ship our Amazon packages!

This also included eating out at places like McDonald's, Starbucks, or anywhere that we went for food that wasn't a grocery store or convenience store.

This was too high, again, this month. It really snuck up on us. Our largest bill was $44 when Craig and I went out in Sedona while my parents watched the kids. It was worth it! The rest had more to do with all of the day-long trips we took, where we packed lunch and then got dinner. We were always careful, and there were some meals where Craig and I would split something then eat more when we got home.

We needed to learn how to spend less at the grocery store to offset eating out when we were out and about a lot. Had to work on that one.

In Summary:

- Business expenses: $588.19
- Groceries: $926.21
- Over by $957.85
- Gas for RV and Car: $657.50
- Campground fees: $46.49
- RV Repairs/Maintenance Car Repairs/Maintenance: $0
- Medical/Pharmacy: $100
- Experiences: $44.37
- Bills: $1561
- Extra Spending/Out To Eat: $975.31

Total: $4881.61

Over again . . .

Why We Were Over Budget

Business expenses were again higher than planned. Gas was more than we thought. It was always hard to predict since we didn't always know where we would be going and how far it was until we got there and figured it out.

We overspent on the extras and eating out. This was normal for us. Again, for the next month, I had to work harder to stay on top of this.

Current Spending - Where we are now

As you can see, we never hit our $4,000 monthly budget, and these were some of our lowest months ever while traveling. Now we are more in the $8,000 - $10,000 a month range. We have been having fun eating out a lot, checking out breweries, doing cool activities, buying things, and staying at campgrounds we want to stay at. As we stated before, we are not doing this lifestyle to save money. We are doing it to travel and enjoy our life.

In Summary

As I have mentioned multiple times, there are various ways you can do this lifestyle. Our biggest recommendation is to put a budget together and then divide it by half and add that half onto your original budget - this is probably more accurate. Unless you are really good at money management - then more power to you!

Now you have some thoughts about what your budget could look like, but how are you going to make money on the road? We will share how we are bringing in an income and different ways other families are making money on the road in the next chapter.

Chapter 4

Making Money On The Road

When we decided to sell our house and move into an RV, we did not have the income part figured out completely.

Our first step was to get out of the house and into the RV. We did this and stayed at a local campground from May to October while Craig went into work, and we figured out how we would make money so we could hit the road and actually travel.

Looking back, I can honestly say I don't know how the heck we actually did this! What if we hadn't figured out how to make money?! What were we going to do?! In October, all the campgrounds near our hometown in Wisconsin shut down for the winter.

We had made about $45,000 when we sold our house, so we knew we had some savings to fall back on. BUT we wanted to travel for the foreseeable future, and that $45,000 would not last long. Through work and focus, it all came together, and we figured out how to get on the road in a roundabout way. . .

Craig would work from home a couple of days a month. Why couldn't he just take his job on the road full time? He worked in IT, so the majority of the work he did could be done remotely. The thing was, no one at his office worked remotely. Luckily, he was really good at what he did, and his boss and colleagues loved him and didn't want him to leave.

Craig approached his boss to ask about the opportunity to work from home 100% of the time. His boss was open to the idea, but they had to take it up the line. It was a whole big process.

It was super stressful while we were waiting and hoping we would get the OK! The day came, and they said yes! I think a big part of this was the kind of employee Craig was and how valuable he was to the team.

But, there was a stipulation. He could be gone for 3 weeks but had to be back for 1 week out of every month. Well, OK, not ideal, but we could travel for those 3 weeks!

We started with that and took off in November for 3 weeks, returned to Wisconsin, and headed out again to Florida. We quickly realized that 3 weeks wasn't enough, so Craig went back in to ask for 8 weeks of remote work before he had to be back.

They said yes again! That meant we could travel farther since we could stay for longer. We ended up getting pretty far south in Florida, and Craig flew back for his 1 week of work while I stayed with the kids in the RV.

After doing this for a while, we noticed 2 things:

- One - we wanted even more freedom, and we didn't want Craig having to sit and work from 9 to 5 every day.
- Two - we didn't want to have to go back anywhere. We wanted total control over our day and schedule.

Throughout this whole time, I worked on starting a Virtual Assistant business and had started to bring on a couple of clients in October before we left Wisconsin. I was also working on building and getting our blog going.

Once we decided we didn't want Craig to have to work for someone anymore, we decided I would focus on my business and build it enough that Craig could leave his job. We set a goal of 6 months for me to build my business to the point that my income would replace Craig's.

This was a crazy time with Craig working all day, and me trying to grow a business while raising 4 kids under the age of 7! I basically gave up sleep for 6 months and would stay up until 2, 3, or 4 in the morning and work when everyone else was sleeping. I also found pockets of time during the day when I could get things done or that Craig could step away for a minute to help with the kids.

Plus, after 5, he would take over so I could focus on working. It was an exciting but stressful time. The cool part was it was working! My business income was increasing, and we were almost at our goal.

At the 5 month mark, I hit it! We were ready for the transition. Or at least we thought we were. Craig went into work and talked to his boss about giving his notice, and his boss asked if he wanted to go down to part-time and we would keep our insurance. Well, hello!! YES, sign us up!!

This meant Craig could continue to work part-time, bring in an income, get us health insurance coverage and allow me more time to work on building my business.

We could not have planned for this, but while making this leap to get on the road and busting our butts, opportunities presented themselves.

By this point, we are about a year and a half into our full-time RV life. Craig continued to work part-time for the next 9 months, and during that time, I continued to build my businesses, Virtual Powerhouse and our Crazy Family Adventure blog.

When Craig was done with his part-time work at Parkside, they wanted him to stay on for 5 hours a week so he could be available to help when things came up. We wouldn't have health insurance, so we had to figure that out (more on this in a future chapter). But it was time to commit more to being entrepreneurs.

Over the years, we continued to focus on growing Virtual

Powerhouse and the Blog. That will lead us into the next part of this chapter, where we share more details on how we were able to bring in six figures while working on the road and traveling full-time with kids.

I wrote the following post a few years ago after we had done all of our taxes and expenses for the year and realized that we had actually brought in 6 figures. If it sounds like we were surprised, we were!

Making 6 Figures From The Road Using Multiple Income Streams

Our entrepreneur journey has been a wild ride and very unplanned and unorganized. Basically, a fake it until you make it or fly by the seat of your pants and figure it out as you go. To be honest, I think that is just how I work, and it was always going to be that way for me.

One of the things we focused on and will continue to focus on is having multiple income streams. It was very obvious to me that in this lifestyle there was a lot of uncertainty and fear. The same paycheck didn't come in every week or month. It varied and was inconsistent.

That is what it means to be an entrepreneur, and for me, the best way to manage this was to have multiple, totally different income streams. This caused challenges since it was basically running multiple businesses. But, it was worth the effort to have some peace of mind about our income.

Three years in, we had a 6 figure income, and didn't even know it was happening! I am a little embarrassed to say we didn't realize we were making that much. When you have multiple streams and no set salary, things can vary, so you don't always have a perfect sense of what is going on.

But hey, I was new to all of this, and sometimes I just had to learn from doing vs. always having my ducks in a row and getting everything 100% right. If I had tried doing that, my business probably never would have started or grown so much! Some of the income went to overhead expenses such as taxes, paying people on the team who do work for my virtual business, video editing for the blog, etc. Our take-home was more around the 60K mark.

We had gone back and forth on how much we needed/wanted for full-time travel and had done it for close to $4k a month but figured that we were falling more into the $5-$7k a month if we wanted to eat out more, stay at some nicer places and do some more expensive activities.

Our goal had always been to only work 20-40 hours a week TOTAL between the 2 of us. Currently, we are close to that at about 20-30 hours each week. We knew we didn't want to work 60-80 hour work weeks when we chose to become entrepreneurs. We chose this lifestyle to spend more time together as a family and to travel.

But getting to this point took more hours than that. Craig was working a full-time 40-hour workweek, and I was working a good 30-40 hours for about 6 months to kick things off so our business could replace his income.

There have been opportunities we had to turn down and choices we had to make to achieve this goal of working less. Had we both continued working 40 hours a week, I truly believe our income would have been doubled. But that was never our goal. Making more money would be great, but we weren't going to give up more time with our kids, and more traveling and exploring to make that happen. Instead, we wanted to learn how to grow our businesses by outsourcing and working.smarter.

Did we think this was possible? Absolutely! Did we know how to do this right away? No. But we worked on it!

Plus, I also understood there would still be weeks where I was working 40 plus hours a week – but I was OK with that since it would be a choice to spend that time working to move things forward with our businesses. The life of an entrepreneur is never consistent!

Stream 1: Virtual Powerhouse (68% of income)

This is the business I began building when we first got on the road. Since then, it has grown to be our largest income stream.

What it was: In simple terms, it was a virtual assistant business. The thing is, when I started, I didn't like the term virtual assistant and didn't like the idea of being an admin/secretary. Instead, I wanted to focus on specific services that I could provide in monthly packages vs. doing hourly work or being on call for whatever a client needed.

What we did: We offered Pinterest strategy/scheduling support, Social Media creating/scheduling, Blog post formatting, email marketing, graphic design, and website design. Yes, that was a lot. And yes, it was multiple streams within one of our streams.

How we did it: I had 5 people working for me. They ranged from an hour a week up to 10-15 hours a week. That was all each person wanted, so it lined up well with what I was looking for and what they were looking for. I thought I might build to have a full-time person on the team in the future, but we weren't there yet.

Craig took on all the website design projects (which came in randomly since it wasn't something we advertised much, instead depending on referrals). My sister, Megan, did all the graphic design work.

Next steps: The potential for this business to grow was there, and I kept trying to figure out how to keep growing it. What I did know was that I definitely wanted to keep focusing on the different streams we had in place in the business, because who knew if Pinterest or Facebook or WordPress would decide to make a drastic change?

Stream 2: Craig's Former 9 to 5 job (18.5% of income)

Craig was in a consultant role with his former business. It was a

Database Administrator role.

What it was: Craig did 5 hours consistently per week of work for them. He also took on projects ranging up to 20 hours a week now and then.

What he did: DBA or database administrator. He helped maintain the databases keeping them current and fine-tuned, and wrote queries so people could pull the data they needed.

How we did it: Craig worked the hours he needed to when he needed to. For this to happen, we needed to be somewhere with internet, and then our kitchen table turned into his office. Or he headed out to the van to do a conference call where it was quieter.

Craig enjoyed the work he was doing and really liked the people he worked with. He also wanted to keep his feet in the industry and keep a pulse on it. The plan was to stay in the consultant role as long as they would have him! Ideally, he worked 5-10 hours a week doing this work.

Stream 3: Crazy Family Adventure Blog (12.5% of income)

Oh, what a journey this has been. You know, when you start traveling full time, you think you can start a blog that is going to make you lots of money . . . the reality is a whole different ball of wax and takes lots of time and dedication to make it a reality!

What it was: We started a blog where we shared family travel destinations, tips, full-time travel, RV travel, and digital nomad information. See that – multiple streams again. We also had a YouTube channel and a Podcast that focused on full-time travel and the journey we were on.

What we did: We tried for the majority of our income to be ad revenue from the blog and some affiliate revenue. We dabbled in sponsored posts but found that we much preferred the more passive income streams of the ads and affiliates. We also did some paid freelance writing.

How we did it: We picked topics to write about that had good keyword density so that we could, hopefully, get on page 1 of searches getting consistent views each day to help with the ad revenue and affiliate sales. For the Podcast and YouTube, we focused on topics and videos that we thought would appeal to our audience and where they would get value out of how this lifestyle worked, and why it was worth traveling with kids.

Next Steps: Our next step was to put more focus on the blog. It had always come #3 behind the streams above, but we would've liked to change that and have it be right up there next to #1 from an income perspective. But the only way to do that was to put more time and effort into it. We had always tried to treat it like a business, but time and resources didn't always allow us to do that. We were currently at over 90,000 unique page views a month, which was super exciting! My goal had always been to get to 100K.

We also wanted to be more consistent with our Podcast and our YouTube channel to continue helping people who want to live a life of full-time family travel.

Stream 4: Courses (1% of income)

We had 3 paid courses and 2 short freebies/opt-ins. Again, multiple streams. See a trend here?!

Course 1: How To Start Your Virtual Business So You Can Travel Full Time

This course gives people the ins and outs of how to start their own business. It shows the exact methods I used to start and grow Virtual Powerhouse. It covers topics like choosing your business, finding clients, networking, and keeping your business simplified.

What We Did: The course is for sale on our site for anyone to purchase whenever they would like. We also have affiliates set up that shared our course with their audience and made a percentage of the sale. Plus, we talked about it on podcasts and wrote about it for other websites.

The course is available on our site:

https://www.crazyfamilyadventure.com/shop/courses/start-virtual-business-course/ Use code BOOK50 to get $50 off the course price!

Course 2: Pinterest and Tailwind 101

This course walked people through the basics of using Pinterest and Tailwind to get more sites to their blog or website. It was a similar strategy that we used with our Pinterest clients. People who didn't want to pay us the monthly fee but, instead, do Pinterest on their own would get all the basic information they needed to get their Pinterest account up and running and to see results!

What we did: Just like course 1, we sold it on our site and through affiliates.

Course 3: Pinterest Pin Image Creation 101

This course walked people through the ins and outs of creating a brand, so their pins were recognizable in the Pinterest news feed. Users would know it was your pin without even seeing your name. It also taught how to create pins in Canva using their pin brand.

What we did: Just like course 1, we sold it on our site and through affiliates.

Course 4: 3 Business Blockers and How to Get Past Them

This is a short FREE email series that talks through the 3 business blockers and how to get past them to build a business and see success.

It is available on the site for free at:

https://www.crazyfamilyadventure.com/shop/courses/3-blockers-can-stop-business-becoming-reality/

Course 5: Pinterest Tips and Tricks

This was a 5 part FREE email series providing tips and tricks for learning more about how to use Pinterest.

There you have it - streams within streams of income. . . . The amazing thing is that all of them continued to grow, and each week, month, and year, we learned more about how to be entrepreneurs. It was a wild, crazy, stressful, and fun ride to be on. Yet, at times I was ready to throw in the towel with all of it and just have Craig get a regular 9 to 5 job again. But then I stopped and realized the freedom we had built and knew I could never go back to a 40 hour   work week lifestyle.

Where Are We Now

Well, that was 3 years ago, so where are we now?!

Stream 1: Virtual Powerhouse

We are still going strong at Virtual Powerhouse, and it continues to grow! I currently have an Operations Manager, A Team Leader, and 7 Strategists on the team. We have switched our main focus over to Pinterest support for small businesses. However, we still do some social media work, and are looking to potentially expand on that. This business is now earning us well over 6 figures a year on its own.

Stream 2: Craig's Job

He is no longer doing any work for his old company. At this point, he has taken on more of the stay-at-home Dad role and the head "teacher" for the kids. While also being the in-house IT support for Virtual Powerhouse and our blog. He will occasionally write blog posts or do YouTube videos as well.

Stream 3: Crazy Family Adventure

Talk about a wild ride! Pre-COVID, our blog was bringing in 300,000 - 375,000 page views a month. You read above that our goal was 100,000. It was so exciting to surpass this by so much!

When COVID hit and travel basically stopped our page views and income dropped by 80%. iI was a mess.

This made us pivot and put more emphasis on paid influencer campaigns. We were able to get our income back to about 70% of where it had been by the end of 2020. Our brand Crazy Family Adventure brings in six figures on its own as well.

Stream 4: Courses

We have stepped away from pursuing more courses. Like I mentioned, you can still purchase our How To Start A Virtual Business Course   here: https://www.crazyfamilyadventure.com/shop/courses/start-virtual-business-course/ There is a lot of great information in it.

The 3 business blockers are still available for free too. We may put together more courses in the future.

Above all else, I was glad that we had Virtual Powerhouse when travel basically crashed. It took a hit as well with COVID but not as much as Crazy Family Adventure did.

We have many other opportunities and things we are working on (this book included), and we are excited to see what the future holds!

Other Opportunities For Making Money

That was our story and how we have been able to stay on the road and build an income. But, it is just 1 of hundreds of ways that you can do this!

I always love how when we meet people on the road; they almost always have a different way of making money. Here are a few examples that we have come across:

- Remote 9 to 5 job
- Graphic Designer
- Vacation Rentals
- Traveling Nurse
- MLM - Plexus, DoTerra, Young Living
- Retired Military
- Amazon Fulfillment Sales
- Living/Traveling Off Of Savings For A Year
- Oil Rig (Spouse leaves for 2 weeks at a time to do this)
- Traveling Construction (family travels and stays where the job is)

There really are so many unique and different ways that people are making money on the road. The opportunities are definitely out there!

What are you thinking? Are you ready? Is this the life for you? The next chapter is all about making the decision!!

Chapter 5

Making The Decision

Alright, the decision has been made. You are doing this?! Holy cow, like for real! You will uproot your whole life and take your family on the road into this unknown but amazing and unbelievable lifestyle. Uhh . . . hmm, how does that make you feel?!

I am guessing excited, nervous, excited, scared, excited, unsure, excited. WOW, can all of those emotions really go through you in a matter of a few seconds? Heck, yeah!

What you are embarking on is life-changing. Yes, life-changing. It is a wild ride, and along with that comes a lot of emotions such as uncertainty, fear and excitement.

When I look back on our decision to actually do this, I remember how exhilarating it was. We are doing something BIG. This isn't just a short trip; this is a whole lifestyle changing, and we are actually doing it.

The focus, feelings, emotions, and excitement are nothing I have ever experienced before - outside of getting married and having kids. It felt so good to have this purpose, this focus, this intention to do something so big and out there.

Along with that came doubt and uncertainty, but the excitement consistently outweighed that. The road to get from a house to an RV was long and a LOT of work. We had a LOT of things. But because our why was so big and so strong, it kept us moving forward.

Looking back, I really can't believe that we did it. How did we do it? Where did we get the energy to do it? How did we not let fear stop us??? Looking back, I can say I'm so proud that we did it. We left an amazing house, neighborhood, community, and extended family to do something courageous and unique with our family.

In reality, it was bumpy then, and it is still bumpy. I remember the emotions of downsizing and feeling like there was no way I was actually going to get everything downsized in time.

Then the actual day when it was time to hand the keys over to the house we had designed and built and thought we would bring grandkids back to - yes, we thought this was the house we would be in for 50 years!

It was also the home we had brought our kids to after they were born. What the heck were we doing?! I didn't think I could hand the keys off to someone else and walk away from this house and never return to it.

Craig told me if we really don't like this new lifestyle, we could always build our old one back up again.

But NOW was the time to go for this - we didn't want to have regrets and look back and wish we hadn't given it a go. So we did it.

Making a decision like this and disrupting your life and your kid's lives shouldn't be taken lightly. It is a big deal, and things will be different. You will be different, and your kids will be different. It will impact all of you in ways that you can't even imagine; some good and some bad.

Once you choose to give this lifestyle a go, you will always know it exists, and it will be hard to go back to your life before. At least that is our take on it, and why we are still doing this 7 years later. We can't imagine not having the freedom and options we have now.

I wanted to share this chapter to let you know that if you, too, are feeling these emotions, you are not alone! It isn't like you chose to do this lifestyle, and now you should be happy, and your life is all of a sudden going to be all rainbows and sunshine and easy. Heck no! It is still life, and there are still emotions and fears. That is all normal.

But once you make the decision, know you are going to have to keep centering yourself on your family's "Why". People will tell you you are crazy, and people aren't going to understand, and it is going to be confusing. But know your "Why" and know your heart and hold strong to that. There will be hard times! But you got this!!

Sharing The News With Friends And Family

OK, you and your partner and kids are excited and you are ready. You can't wait to kick everything off! But now you need to tell your family and friends . . . this could really go a lot of ways.

In our case, we had always been a little out there with things we did. So when we shared that we were going to do this, everyone was kind of like, hmm, interesting. OK, sounds good. I thought some of them thought we couldn't or wouldn't actually do it. While others couldn't fathom that this could actually be a way to live.

We were lucky, and no one really pushed back on us. Both our parents knew we were determined, and nothing they said would change our minds. So they supported us - which was amazing.

Our friends also supported what we were doing and were curious to see how it went. We had a few friends that thought it sounded amazing, but were happy in their box, and said they would stay and watch us live outside the box. At least they knew what they wanted!

As the months went on and the reality set in, and people saw us actually doing it, they became more supportive. It was exciting to share what we were doing and to have their support!

A few months into us hitting the road, my Mom told my Dad they needed an RV if we would be doing this (remember, my sister was doing it, too!). My Dad said no. My Mom said yes and went out and found a truck and a fifth wheel for sale and told my Dad she would learn how to do everything with it. So they showed up and camped with us multiple times that first summer!

Now my parents are also full-time RVers! My Dad is on board and loves it, and they have been traveling full time in an RV for years. We spend a lot of time with them on the road, which is great.

I asked them about a year ago if they regretted the decision to live this way, and they said 100% no. Choosing this lifestyle actually made them closer as a couple and they love living this way!

They have been through 2 knee surgeries for my Mom and a quadruple bypass for my Dad, all while living in the RV. They have also hiked to the tops of mountains with us and explored Baja, Mexico and Canada.

Now, this is obviously an extreme response and one for which we are so thankful. Craig's parents are also great and always have a spot for us to come and stay in their driveway back in our hometown! Even that has been great and has allowed us to spend a lot of time with them - versus just coming over a few times a month to hang out. Now we are there for weeks at a time and spend a lot of quality time together.

This isn't always the response people get when they hit the road. We understand that. If you have friends and family that aren't supportive, it can be hard. But this is your family and your life and your choice. My guess is they will come around to it when they see how much fun you are having and how much you and your family are thriving!

That being said, you may want to acknowledge their fears. They may have some good points and things you want to look into. Also, just answering their questions, explaining your plan, and sharing your why may help alleviate their fears and get them excited right along with you!

I also think this pushback can come from a place of love and fear of them losing so much time with you. Especially if you live close to them and they are used to seeing you a lot. They may be worried you will miss all the holidays or that they will only see you once a year. These are all good conversations to have to get everyone on the same page.

It could be an easy conversation, or it could be hard, but it needs to happen, and you should be prepared for it to go either way. But in the end, you know what you want and what you want to do!

Up next: Picking the RV for your family! In the next chapter, we share each rig we have been in and what we liked and didn't like about them, and what we think are the most important things to think about when looking at RVs.

Chapter 6

Picking Your Rig

Picking the right family RV can definitely be a challenge! There are so many options, from drivable to towables and different lengths, sizes and layouts. We have had 6 different rigs - 5 of them we lived full-time in. We hope our insights and tips can help you figure out which rig is right for you and your family.

Below we share our list of things to consider, and then after that, we share the 6 rigs we have been in and the pros and cons of each.

Style Of Travel And Life

This is the most important thing to consider when looking for the right rig for your family. This can change the longer you are on the road, or because of your kids' age, etc.

How Fast Will You Be Moving?

Do you plan to stay in one place for weeks to months at a time? Or do you plan to move quickly, only staying at places for 3-5 nights?

If you plan to stay at locations for weeks/months at a time, you may want to go bigger with your rig. It is definitely nice to have space to spread out, and if you are at one place for a long stretch, you can really get settled in, and your rig can feel just like a small apartment!

If you plan to move quickly from place to place, a smaller rig with fewer things and setup may be the way to go.

What Seasons Will You Travel In?

Are you planning to do a lot of winter or summer travel? If yes, you definitely want to take weather into account. Planning to be in colder climates for a lot of the year? You will then want to look at a 4 season type of rig or something with heated tanks and underbelly. Without this, it can get really stressful, and/or you will have to do a lot of prep work.

Actually, not even 4 seasons RVs are really made for winter weather - so if you plan on a lot of winter weather you will have to do some additional work on your rig.

If you plan to travel a lot to hot places like 90 - 100 degrees, know that your RV AC unit can really only get the rig down about 20% from the outside temperature. For this reason, you may want to look for a rig with 2 ACs so, at least, you have a bit more AC power.

Where Will You Stay?

Do you want to stay just at campgrounds with full hookups and easy in and out access, or do you want to do more National Parks, State Parks, and boondocking (staying without hookups on BLM land and other places)?

Campgrounds

If you are looking for mostly full hookup campgrounds like KOAs, then a bigger rig will work just fine - though with a smaller rig, you have more options for sites and availability - so something to consider. Also consider cost, since KOAs are expensive.

National/State Parks

If you want to do more National and State Parks where you are staying in the parks, we recommend going with a smaller rig. Yes, they do sometimes have spots for larger rigs, but more often than not, they don't.

If you don't think you want to go under 30 feet, then we would recommend staying as close to 35/36 feet as you can.

When we stayed in the Smoky Mountains National Park, you had to be 35 feet or under to stay (you are usually OK in these spots with a 36-foot rig, too).

On the west coast, the National and State parks are even smaller. If you really prefer this kind of travel then going smaller makes a lot of sense.

Boondocking

If you are interested in boondocking a lot, you can definitely do this with a bigger rig, but again, you will be limited since many boondocking spots are made for rigs 30 feet and under. This doesn't mean you can't find spots for larger rigs. You definitely can - but they can be harder to find. A bigger rig can have a more difficult time accessing boondocking spots since they are often off the beaten path and access can be very bumpy.

Another thing to consider if you plan on Boondocking is space for solar panels on the roof, space for more or better batteries, and having a generator. All rigs can boondock, but there are definitely things that you need to have in place to make it enjoyable.

Work/Homeschooling Schedule

Does someone in the family have to work a 9 to 5 job? Are you planning to do strict/consistent homeschooling with your kids?

If someone in the family is working a 9 to 5 job and one spouse is home with the kids all day, you will probably want a bigger rig unless you are OK spending a lot of time outside or having one spouse take the kids out exploring while the other one is working.

If you need an office space and/or a quiet spot for multiple calls a day, then a bigger rig may make more sense.

The same goes if you will be doing a very consistent and strict homeschooling schedule and potentially have a lot of books and supplies. More room is beneficial for this.

If you plan to travel faster and don't have as much of a work restriction and plan to unschool or have a more flexible daily schedule, a smaller rig may work better.

Where To Buy Your Family RV

There are a couple of things to think about when you are deciding where to buy your RV. Ideally, you can purchase from a place that also offers RV service because, let's face it, things break on RVs, and you will have to bring it in at some point. Second, picking an RV dealer that has locations around the US is great because when you need service on your trip, going to the same dealership you bought it from is a great feeling. This is especially important if you are going full-time. Who knows where you will be when something goes wrong.

We bought two rigs via RV Trader/private sale, one via a small RV dealership (this did not go well) and the other one at a local dealer near our hometown. Then for the last 2, we went to Camping World. We did this for a few reasons.

One, we like that Camping World is a one-stop-shop for all your RVing needs. They really have everything you would ever need for your RV, as well as so many cute RV-themed cups, rugs, tablecloths, etc.!

They have a smooth and easy trade-in process, which we have used both times. Seriously, it was so easy - basically, get a quote on your trade-in value just by filling out a piece of paper (no need to bring the rig in). Then when it is time to trade it in, you sign a few papers, bring the RV in, move your things from your old RV to your new RV, give them the keys, and you are done!

We have also been pleased with their sales team each time we have visited (we have been to multiple locations on our travels). Their prices are usually competitive compared to what we find online and in other places. They almost always have large selections of RVs, and their websites are pretty up to date with their inventory.

Based on our experience, we would recommend buying an RV from Camping World.

Cargo Capacity

If you take anything away from this, let it be this - know your weights! Cargo Capacity is the amount of weight your rig can handle for all of your things, water, filled tanks, etc. We have concluded that for RV living, especially full-time travel with kids, you want as close to 4,000 pounds cargo capacity as you can get.

Take note that this is not easy to find in towable rigs. For Class A's/C's, it can be easier. Our current rig has 3,700lbs cargo capacity. . . yes, we would have preferred a few hundred more, but figured we would make this one work.

You can try to tell yourself you don't have that much stuff, or you will get rid of things. But please believe us when we say the weight piles up quickly! Even just a trip to the grocery store adds a couple hundred pounds. Clothes weigh more than you think . . . and outside gear can get heavy.

In any case, we highly recommend aiming for 3500-4000+ pounds for Cargo Capacity if you will be going full time in the rig - and don't forget to take this into account as you find your tow vehicle if you are going with a towable.

If you plan to add solar and a boondocking setup, don't forget to consider how much the panels, batteries and generator will weigh. I told you it adds up fast!

Age Of Kids

I do think the age of your kids can be a factor in picking your rig. When kids are little, they want to be around you anyways, and you normally have to keep an eye on them, so having a small space is fine.

The same goes for sleeping - they are usually heavier sleepers or sleep for longer stretches, so if they are close to their parents' bed, it is OK.

As kids get older, they definitely want more room to spread out, set up their own decorations, computers, etc. They also tend to sleep less or stay up later, and parents usually prefer more privacy from curious ears and eyes!

That being said, if this is a vacation rig or you are just making a year-long trip, then all the kids really need is a place to sleep. They will adjust to everything else.

Also, kids are very adaptable, so they will handle things better than the parents and will be able to adjust to the space.

Amount of Kids/Guest Visitor

If you have many kids or plan on having a lot of guests/visitors in your rig, you may want something with more space. As an example, if we only had 2 kids, we would have a smaller rig. Having 4 kids means we need more beds and just overall more space in our living area. Yes, we have had tiny spaces and made it work, but most people with a bigger family thought we were crazy.

If Grandma and Grandpa, or other family and friends, plan to visit and stay in your rig you will want to make sure they have somewhere to stay. It can just be a fold-down couch or table, but again, something to consider.

Comfort of Driving

Before getting a massive rig or deciding between towing or getting a driveable, you will want to consider your comfort level with driving. Towing something, especially a trailer, is not easy and can be a learning curve. If you have already done it a lot or don't get stressed about situations like this, you will figure it out.

In our opinion, a Class C is the easiest to get used to - since it is more like driving a truck down the road than any other option. But if you get a 35 foot Class C, it may not feel this way. Craig enjoyed driving the Class A - except that it was so big, so you couldn't just randomly stop somewhere very easily.

He would say a 5th wheel is definitely way easier to tow than a trailer from a towing perspective! If you want something longer than 24 feet, then he would recommend the 5th wheel, hands down.

Not A Home

You can (and should) give up some things to get the rig you want. Do you need 2 bathrooms? Do you need a big bed? What are your essentials? What do you really need to have? We think a 36-foot rig with 1 bathroom is a better choice than a 42-foot rig with 2 bathrooms.

This is not a home, so it won't have everything, but that is 100% OK, and we can promise - you will adjust! So, put together a list of your must-haves and then reevaluate and determine what is really a must-have and what is nice to have. Be strict about it and set realistic expectations.

Traveling the way you want and getting into the places you want to is way better than having everything you need in your rig.

Note that all of the above can change while traveling, especially if you plan to be on the road for years.

Which is why we have been in 5 rigs since going full- time. When we started, we wanted more space as we moved from a big house to an RV. After that, we wanted to go smaller to travel easier to the places we wanted to go and not be limited by size. Then we wanted to go back to having more space as the kids got older.

Below we share the rigs we have been in and the benefits and downsides of each.

1st Rig (non-full-time) – 29-foot Jayco (Class C)

Before we started traveling full time, we had a 29-foot Jayco Jamboree Class C. It had 4 bunks in the back but no slideouts, so we thought we needed something bigger when we decided to go full-time. So, we sold that one and bought a 39-foot Class A Diesel Pusher.

This rig was great since it was a smaller size, and we could easily get around places. Plus, a Class C is much more like driving a pickup truck or big van, so it was a good first rig to have.

2nd Rig – 39-foot Newmar Diesel Pusher Motorhome - 3910 Kountry Star (Class A)

When we started full-time travel, we had a 39-foot Diesel pusher motorhome (3910 Newmar Kountry Star and towed a GMC Acadia), and we actually remodeled the back room so that all 6 of our beds were back there. When the kids were 6, 4, 4, and 2, this worked out great! Mom and Dad just shut the door and used the living room for private space at night.

It was nice to have a big rig, and we definitely didn't realize some of the really nice things about it and how high quality the Newmar was - until we sold it! The RV had 4 slideouts, so it was huge once we opened it up. Plus, it had a lot of storage both inside and outside. And we didn't have to worry about the cargo-carrying capacity at all!

Benefits of a Class A:

- Drive days are really comfortable!
- If someone had to use the bathroom, they could (other than Craig who was driving). This was great - especially with younger kids!
- You could grab food whenever you wanted—no need to pack snacks for the trip.
- The kids had a huge TV to watch movies on while we were traveling.
- Storage
- The Diesel Pusher has a lot of power and is built like a semi, so

we didn't even think about the cargo capacity.

- There was a lot of storage and cabinets in the rig.
- There is a ton of pass-through storage in the rig's basement, and I mean a TON. You don't get that in towables.
- We could tow a regular car/SUV versus having to have a big truck.

The downside of a Class A:

- We were very concerned that if something broke, it would be costly to fix.
- Drive days were easier, but securing car seats wasn't ideal. We did have a seat belt for each seat, but it was definitely not as secure as in a car/truck. Plus, you had to move the car seats from the car to the rig on travel days.
- The layouts are limited. You really can't find any with 2 bedrooms or even regular beds for 6 people (unless they are huge rigs).
- We really enjoyed the space with the rig and all of the benefits, but we started not liking being so big driving down the road. We were basically the same size as semi-trucks! Making random roadside stops either wasn't possible or was very stressful.
- Also, when towing a car, you can't really back up ... so you don't want to get stuck in a situation like that. You would have to unhook the towed vehicle in the middle of the road so you can turn around.

3rd Rig – 23-foot Winnebago View 23J

RVing by Banff National Park

We decided to downsize and went for a 23-foot Winnebago View Class C for our next rig. Yes, it was tiny, especially for 6 people and 2 big dogs! But we were anxious to get smaller and to try traveling without a car.

Benefits of a Class C:

- You get the extra space above the driver area, which makes it almost like 2 bedrooms.
- When driving it, it feels more like a regular truck. This is the only rig I have driven on the highway since I felt like I could handle it.
- We were so small we could fit into a parking spot at the grocery store.

Downsides of a Class C:

- Cargo Capacity - we had to take into account our things and water and gas and us since we would be driving in the rig. There just wasn't enough cargo capacity in the smaller one we bought.
- I didn't like how the car seats had to be installed. They were just in the booth in the rig. They did each have a seatbelt to secure the

seats in but not as secure as in a car/truck. And we had to move them when we got to places to use the booth area.

- Part of why we switched to this one was to avoid major repairs . . . well, right after we got it, we ended up having a lot of issues. This pushed us to switch to a new rig.
- Needless to say, this ended up not being the right option for us. That being said, we did have a lot of fun with this rig and took it up to Canada to explore Banff and Jasper, and it was a great rig for that!

4th Rig – 21-foot Micro Minnie Travel Trailer

This time we wanted to try a brand new rig (after dealing with all of the issues with the pre-owned Class C) and opted for a 21-foot travel trailer and a 12 passenger van. We went with the Winnebago Micro Minnie 2100BH.

The thought was we could also remodel the van if we wanted to and use that for off-road trips (we never did this, but liked the idea of being able to).

Right after we bought this new setup, we headed straight down to Baja, Mexico! It was a great setup for that since we were so small it was easy to get to any of the places we wanted to go. And at 21 feet long and

7 feet wide, we fit into all of the RV parks down there.

The Van was a 12 passenger Chevy Express 3500 (6L).

Benefits of a 21-foot travel trailer

- Even at just 21 feet, we could get a decent layout for our family.
- Car seats were now properly installed and secured in the van.
- We were still small enough to fit into grocery store parking lots easily and anywhere else we wanted to go.
- It was great having the big 12 passenger van for our vehicle. We could use it for storage, and there was a lot of room for the kids to spread out. Plus we could take a few other people along with us when we went places.
- The rig also had over 3000lb's of cargo capacity.
- Having the smaller trailer meant the van could easily handle this size rig. This is probably the least stressed that Craig has been while driving any of our rigs.

Downsides of a 21-foot Travel Trailer:

- It was tiny, so there wasn't really any way to comfortably all hang out inside. Which was actually fine with us and we spent a lot of time outside - if the weather is right and there isn't a lot of rain, this is great!
- This was a great setup for many reasons, and then a few people in the family started to outgrow it. Craig wanted a bigger kitchen and more space, and Carson, our oldest, just wanted more room. It all made sense, so we decided to move to a 30-foot trailer.

5th rig – 30-foot Jayco JayFlight 267BHSW Baja/Rocky Mountain Edition Travel Trailer

We didn't want to go the 5th wheel route as we were hoping we could keep the van and use that to tow the trailer. Our choice was a 30-foot Jayco 267BHSW Baja/Rocky Mountain Travel Trailer. Unfortunately, we quickly learned that wasn't going to be the case. The van (a 12 passenger Chevy Express 3500 (6L)) really didn't handle the 30-foot trailer well at all. . . we dealt with it for a while and then traded the van in for a Ford F350 diesel single rear wheel short bed truck.

We wanted this one since it had a higher suspension and bigger wheels, so we could easily take it boondocking and off-road. The Minnie Winnie was really low to the ground, so we were excited about this!

Benefits of the 30-foot Travel Trailer:

- The inside layout was really nice. It had a bedroom for Craig and me and then a full-size double bunk for the kids in the corner. You could really fit a lot of living space in this trailer.
- It is cheaper than a fifth wheel or motorized rig.

Downsides of the 30-foot Travel Trailer:

- It wasn't super durable inside - which is a problem with kids.
- The Cargo Capacity was nowhere near what we needed it to be. So even though it had space for all of our things, weight-wise it couldn't handle it.
- We couldn't safely tow it with the van, so we had to get a truck.
- Towing a 30-foot trailer was the most stressed that Craig has been with driving any of our setups. This could have been due to the higher suspension, bigger wheels, and regular Goodyear Wrangler off-road tires, giving it a higher center of gravity and more prone to sway.

6th Rig - 36-foot 5th Wheel

The downsides led us to want to try something else, and we were excited to try out a fifth wheel! We now had the truck, so that was good. We did a lot of research and knew we still wanted to stay smaller - ideally 35 feet or under. But we still wanted a bedroom space for the kids.

We came across the Montana High Country 335BH, and it was a great fit! Thirty-six feet long with a slide-out in the back to make a small bedroom for the kids! Plus a loft area. And we would have a king-sized bed!

We had the Ford F350 diesel single rear wheel short bed truck that could tow the 5th wheel so that was all set.

With being 36 feet and part of it going over the truck, it really didn't make us that much longer than the 30-foot trailer, so that was a bonus. We also heard it was much easier to tow than a trailer.

Benefits of the 5th wheel:

- Much easier to tow than the trailer. Craig couldn't believe how much easier and better it felt!
- It has an excellent layout with a big fridge, 2 bedrooms, a loft area, and a big living room area. 5th wheels lend themselves to more of an apartment-style layout.
- We intentionally got one that had a cargo capacity between 3000 - 4000 pounds.

Downsides of the 5th Wheel:

- It is still 36 feet. This isn't really a downside per se, but there are times we miss having our tiny 21-foot trailer just because it was so easy to travel with!
- We don't have a bathroom in the truck, so having to stop when people have to go to the bathroom can be annoying.
- We can access our fridge when the slide-outs are in but not the cabinets, so we have to do some pre-planning for travel days.

Needless to say, there are benefits and downsides to all of the rigs we have been in. We have concluded that there isn't a perfect rig for full-time family travel. However, there are many things to consider so you can get the right rig for your season of travel and life. When we went looking for our 6th rig, we put together a list of our must-haves based on the experiences we had from the last 5 rigs. Here is what we came up with (for a family of 6 with 4 kids ages 12,10,10, and 8).

Our Must-Have List

This is the list we put together before we bought our 6th rig listed above. Please note this list is VERY different than the one from our first year of travel and has a lot of choices based on 6 years of being on the road and being ready for more space and more luxuries. If we made this list when we first started, then the only thing that would be on here is Cargo Capacity.

BIG Fridge

For all of our years on the road, we have always had an RV size fridge. Yes, it was doable, but, it was frustrating, too. This time, we knew we wanted to give a big fridge a try, and let me tell you - it is fabulous.

Cargo Capacity

We knew we wanted a cargo capacity of 3500 or more. Ideally, this would be 4000 or more, but you can't really find those in the size we were looking for.

We had to be in the right weight range to work with our current truck - we didn't want to have to get another.

Kids Room Area

We wanted a bedroom area for the kids where they could set up their computers and gaming systems. When our kids were little, I didn't think this was as important at all. They were fine playing in the common space and preferred that.

As they have gotten older and into gaming, they really wanted a space where they could set up their systems and leave them set up versus setting them up at the kitchen table and having to take it down every night.

P.S. We have been on the road for 6 years, so this is life to us. If you plan on only being on the road for 1 year, I don't think you need to worry as much about a gaming space or separate bedroom area for the kids.

Kids beds

We wanted a separate bed area for each kid that they could decorate and have as their own. Our kids hadn't had a problem sharing a bed from a sleeping perspective, and I think they do miss it now. It can be lonely sleeping in your own bed!

But from a "my" space idea and freedom to decorate how they wanted to, it is nice that they each have their own space. Our daughter definitely cares more about this than the boys, though.

Things To Keep In Mind

Here is a recap of the top things we think you should keep in mind when you are looking for the right rig for your family:

Cargo Capacity

This is HUGE for full-time travel - I can't say this enough! We can tell you that with 6 people in our family, our stuff plus water and sewer (yes, sometimes we travel with these empty, but there are also a lot of times when you need water or aren't able to dump - like when boondocking.) You will want to have a Cargo Capacity close to 4,000lbs. Your stuff weighs more than you think (this is pretty much everything you own when you hit the road.) Things like groceries and water weight add up really fast.

This is why a motorhome may be a smart option for your family as well. They usually have a higher cargo capacity - especially diesel pushers.

Travel Style/Rig Size

Give this some thought before making your choice. The size of your rig does matter and can impact how you travel. Don't just get pulled in by a massive floor plan you see at the RV dealership. Yes, it looks great just sitting there. But when you are towing it down the road or looking for campsites, you may not like it as much...

Have this conversation with your family to really determine what the goals are when you hit the road. How do you want to travel, what will daily life look like, what will work-life and homeschool life look like?

Towing Vehicle

Your towing vehicle has to be able to handle your rig weight-wise. If it doesn't, towing will be super stressful, dangerous even, and you don't want that! Learn everything you can about weights and what your truck can tow - this is actually pretty complicated, and it isn't just one number.

You need to know the tongue or pin weight, the truck GVWR, truck axle weight ratings, the rig weight, and probably something else I am forgetting. Take your time to really understand this BEFORE you buy your truck or rig. People have said it's a good idea to find the rig you want first. Then you know exactly how much it weighs before getting the tow vehicle for it. Then you can get the tow vehicle that is right for your rig.

Food storage

We went for 6 years with a regular size RV fridge. It is workable but annoying—your call on how you want to handle this. We also have a big pantry now for dry food storage. This is great and something we haven't had in a while!

Sleeping

Our kids have shared beds for a long time, and it was fine. Now that our oldest is 13, we are hitting the phase where we feel it is more important for him to have his own space. But really, he had no issue sleeping in the same bed with his little brother. A lot of times, we would find them snuggling in bed in the morning. So we didn't really have to do this for that reason. And I loved how sharing a bed made them all closer!

Extras that are really nice to have, but not imperative:

Please note, I would not recommend any of these if it meant we had to be 40 feet long. Being smaller and the flexibility it gives us is so much more important!

Washer/Dryer

We went years without one, and it was fine. But it is nice to have one!

Fireplace

I would NEVER have said this is a nice thing to have and thought they were wasted space. Now that we have one, I LOVE it on cold nights or mornings!

All in all, we don't think there is a perfect rig for full-time family travel. Instead, there are different choices for the different reasons you are traveling, ages of kids, work/school life, etc. Also, remember this does not need to be your last rig. You can see we have changed multiple times. It is better to pick something and get on the road rather than let this hold you up. As you can tell, we have gone from big to small and then back to big.

Here's an article we wrote when we went from our 39-foot motorhome down to a 23-foot Class C.

Why We Downsized Our RV

When you go from a 2700+ square foot house into an RV full-time, you think you need a LOT of space in your RV. Which prompted us to look at 39 to 45 foot RVs when we decided to go full-time.

Before that, we had owned a 29-foot class C for about 4 months, but that felt way too small for us. Which is why we bought a 39 foot Diesel Pusher Motorhome.

Challenges of a Bigger Rig

- If something went wrong with this one, it was going to cost us thousands of dollars to fix. The tires alone cost over $4K. This started to get a little scary the longer we lived in it.
- We wanted to do more boondocking, which we did with the 39-footer. But we never wanted to go too far off the beaten path since we didn't want to get in a situation where we couldn't get out of. Or we didn't want to get stuck and have to get it towed out!
- This always made us hesitant to try any boondocking sites unless we knew big rigs could easily fit.
- When we left somewhere, we NEVER wanted to make an unexpected stop since, again, we were concerned about getting stuck, taking a wrong turn, hitting a low bridge, the list goes on and on. Basically, it was a matter of getting from point A to B with the least number of stops possible.
- Gas stations. The only ones that really work with a rig that big are truck stops. They work great for big rigs, but they aren't always easy to find, and even when you do find them, it is always stressful getting in and out.
- We found ourselves spending days at a time inside the RV without ever going outside. It almost felt like it was an effort to get outside - crazy, right?! But it really was like an apartment on wheels.

All of these reasons led us to start considering downsizing. But we never planned on ending up in a 23-foot rig! Our original thought was to go around 26 feet with a full walk-around queen size bed in the back that we could convert to a king bed and put a bunk bed above it.

We looked and found a few options but started thinking if we were going to do this, let's go all in. However, a van was not an option with the 4 kids and 2 dogs. We would have loved a Westfalia, but that felt too extreme.

Then we started looking into the Winnebago View, which is built on a Sprinter chassis. That means it is basically as wide as a van - so we can fit in any parking spot! With the length being 23 foot we would be just like a big dually truck and would be able to park almost anywhere.

I still wasn't sold on it - I mean 23 feet and 1 slide-out for 6 people and 2 big dogs didn't seem feasible. But Craig was in love with the View since it looked like a fun little toy, and he really liked the 2006 model and color scheme (which matches our logo - I swear we didn't plan on that!). I started to come around and really consider how we could make it work.

We came up with a plan to take the back corner bed and turn it into bunks—2 kids on each. Craig and I would sleep above the cab, which would still give us some privacy when the kids went to sleep at night.

We decided we wanted a 2006 Winnebago View! We started looking and came across a few and found out that it would not be able to tow our car since it weighed almost 5K pounds and the View can only tow around 3500. We bought a View and kept our car. We discussed trying to find a lighter car that we could potentially tow - but there weren't many options for light vehicles that could fit 6 people and 2 dogs!

When we had the View I would follow Craig with the car. Yes, 2 engines, double the gas, and I lost my work time I used to have when we were traveling. But we were working on a solution. If there is one thing this life has taught us is to be flexible.

Other than that, I can honestly say that at night, when everyone was sleeping and Craig and I got a chance to take a breath and really think about where we were at, we were pleased and content with our decision. It just felt right. We are spending a lot more time outside and even just being in the rig felt more like we are camping or living outside.

We figured out little storage options and places for all of our stuff to fit. We even found a spot for our Berkey on the counter!

It felt right. The kids didn't skip a beat and adjusted. The dogs had a harder time finding their place in the new rig, but it got better every day.

We never ended up getting a different car and instead I followed in the car and when we headed to Canada we dropped the car off at Craig's parents so we could all ride together in the RV.

As you read above this ended up not being the best rig and we were way over weight for it and it has tons of mechanical issues . . . sometimes that happens. Live and learn! It didn't stop us from wanting to stay small though as our next rig was the 21 foot trailer.

What We Found Out From Downsizing Our RV

- Ease of travel. 23 feet is a whole lot easier to pull into a grocery store parking lot, make a random stop at a farm stand, or turn around if we took a wrong turn!
- Campsites. When you call and say we are looking for a 23-foot rig site, there are normally a lot of options! With a 39-footer, not so much.
- National and State Parks. We could stay at all of the National and State Parks. In the 39-footer, that wasn't possible. With 23 feet, there were no limitations for us.
- Boondocking. We felt much more comfortable getting adventurous in this rig and maybe getting ourselves in situations where we would never have fit or been able to get out with the bigger rig.
- Being outside. We were excited to spend more time outside and love that the outside now felt like part of our living space since the rig is lower to the ground and the door was right there. It really felt like the outside was part of our living space.

Take note we stayed downsized for a few years and were ready to move up to something larger after that. The reality is there is no perfect rig BUT there are rigs that are right for that season of travel, kids ages, work, etc.

Up next: Ok, you found a rig! Now it is time to figure out how to downsize and move into your RV! Let's do this!!

Chapter 7

Downsizing

When we launched, we downsized from a 2700+ sq foot house to fit into a 39-foot motorhome. The process took us about nine months from start to finish. I don't think there is a set amount of time that it should take you to downsize. It more has to do with how much time you have and making that work.

Downsizing all of your things is not an easy task. In this chapter, we will share tips to help you downsize and prepare for full-time RV travel.

The first part of downsizing is asking yourself if you are ready to sell it all.

Do you want to get rid of your beds, furniture, TV, and not have anything but what is in the RV with you?

Or are you planning on renting your house out or getting a large storage unit where you could put all or some of these things so that you would still have them?

Things to Consider When Downsizing:

- Getting a storage unit could cost you a hundred dollars or so a month.
- If you have these things back in your hometown, they will still be taking up that space in your head.

- Do you want to keep all of it, or do you want to wipe the slate clean and go for it??
- Do you want to get a storage shed to keep your things in case you change your mind about full-time travel after a few months?
- Or maybe you have a lot of really nice furniture that you have spent a lot of money on so you don't want to get rid of it.
- Do your future plans include buying a house again?

These are all things to consider. In our case, we decided to go for it and get rid of it all.

For us, it made total sense, and 6 years later, we haven't looked back and wished we would have kept any of it.

Downsizing is a process both mentally and physically. I did buy a couple of books on simplifying and minimizing your life to get a few ideas and get my head in the right space.

Usually, I just jump in and start doing and then learn as I'm going - I never did finish any of the books, but there were some good tips in them. So here's what we learned from the process, and I would say it's probably about a five-round process.

Round One

You jump in and get rid of all those things that you've always wanted to get rid of, and you just never took the time to do. This first round is pretty easy. Yes, it takes time, but there isn't a lot of decision-making since these are all the things you knew you wanted to get rid of anyways.

This is also the round where you really stop and look around at all of your things. Look for the dust that shows you haven't used it or cared enough to clean it in a long time which probably means you don't need it. Or if you open a drawer and realize you haven't touched anything in the drawer for a whole year which means you don't need it.

It is about opening your eyes and really seeing all of the things that you have.

In this round, I would also recommend talking to your kids about what you are doing - no matter how old they are. This will help them realize what is happening and prepare them for downsizing their clothes, books, toys and things.

Talk to your kids about picking their 3 favorite toys they want to bring with them (we carried around this gigantic plastic dinosaur for years!) Then, their 5 favorite books and their favorite outfit. Or something like that. Keep them involved in the process.

As you go through each round, never throw away or get rid of your kids' things without asking them first. Could you imagine the confusion if they woke up one morning and half their toys were gone!

You will be surprised that when you ask your kids if they want to get rid of something, more often than not, they say yes. They usually have less attachment to their things than we do as parents.

If you have a kid that does push back a lot, spend some time talking to them about what you are doing and why you are doing it and be very careful to keep them involved. Don't try to sneak things out without them knowing.Believe me, they know or will figure it out, and that won't be good for your relationship with them or the trust level they have with you.

Honestly, getting the kids on board was easy, and it wasn't difficult to do this with them. At one point, one of the kids said to me, "Mommy; I don't really care. You take care of it." If they come to that decision on their own, they are much more accepting of what needs to be done.

I had a harder time letting go of their toys and the memories they brought me than they did!

Round Two

Round one is pretty easy. Round 2 is a little more difficult. When you look around, you realize you are still saving the newborn clothes because, you know, maybe someone will want them someday. Or your old college textbooks - because maybe you will want to look at them again or use them (right, right).

When you have a house and space for things like this, you end up just keeping them. Because you can. Well, guess what? In an RV you can't! It's time to figure out what to do with these things. So round two is about diving into what we've thought about getting rid of but haven't taken action on.

There were things I went through and knew I wasn't ready to get rid of just yet. So I pushed it off until the next round. And there were some whole rooms like our basement storage and the office closet that were filled with old papers and books that I wasn't ready to touch.

That's OK - that is why there are 5 rounds. If there are things you want to push off, push them off for now - there will come a time when you can't push them off anymore! But that time isn't now.

Time to start making some of those decisions and figuring out what you will do with the things. Will you sell them? Donate them? Throw them away? Give them to a friend?

We used Facebook a lot and found local garage sale pages where we could sell things. I would not recommend doing this for everything, but for large items or items that are worth something, it is worth it.

We would put a whole bag of baby clothes together and list it for $10 for the bag. We found that if people don't comment right away, you probably aren't going to sell whatever you posted. So be ready to lower the price by a lot or donate it. This will also show you that things you may feel are worth money aren't worth much to other people. That can be hard to swallow. But be ready for it. The goal here isn't to make a ton of money but instead, downsize and get ready for your adventure!

We also had 2 rummage sales. One at our house. That took a lot of time, and we didn't even sell that much! I'll talk about the second sale below.

I can't even remember the number of trips we took to Goodwill. But it was a lot. We also gave many nicer toys away to friends that we knew would enjoy them and use them.

Round Three

Time to tackle the things you don't really want to do. These, again, aren't emotionally hard things, but more just things that need to get done and will be tedious. Time to sit down and go through that office paperwork. Next up is tackling the basement storage you haven't gone through in years.

As much as you can, get rid of it. Or put it aside for the Round 4 garage sale.

This can be a hard round since you are starting to hit the point that you can't ignore these areas or things that need to be gone through. This is the boring stuff that you just kept ignoring and telling yourself you would eventually get to over the years. Well, now is the time!

Set a timer for 30 minutes or an hour and work, work, work to get through these areas!

Round Four

We are getting to the end! Time to move the majority of things out. We tried one rummage sale that didn't go so well - 4 people showed up! The second time around, we picked a better location. It was my sister's house, which was on a busy street and was known for being a good rummage sale location.

It was time to move anything out that we thought we could make some money from. We figured after this; we would be donating things.

For this rummage sale, we had about 100 people come through. We didn't put prices on anything, but instead, put it all out and told people to name a price for the whole pile of things they wanted.

We did the rummage sale for 2 days. The second day it started to rain, so we packed everything up and donated it. NOT 1 THING CAME HOME WITH US. This is an important thing to note. We didn't bring anything home from the rummage sale. It all was sold or donated—end of story.

When preparing for the rummage sale, you can set aside 3 areas or baskets. One area will be things you want to keep; the second area/basket are things you aren't sure about. The third area will be things you know are going to the rummage sale.

Once you have broken everything down this way, it is time to go back through it and see if anything can move from area 1 or 2 into 3. Go through this 2 or 3 times to make sure you have moved everything you can to area 3 for the rummage sale. Remember, there is only 1 more round after this! Time to really narrow things down!

Fifth and Final Round

Last round! This is the round that you say - OK, I need to make some tough choices. Things from the first 4 rounds that we never thought we could get rid of or kept putting off. We realize we just don't have the room and have to get rid of them.

Each round, I felt like my comfort zone was stretching a little bit farther to where I could get rid of more and more things. I will say that now that we have gone through this and it is six years later; there has not been one thing that we wish we would have kept. And remember, if there is something you get rid of and a month or so later you really want it - you can always go out and buy it again.

It definitely starts to feel very freeing as you let things go and get rid of so many things you really didn't need. But don't let any of this mislead you. It is a very hard process to go through. Emotionally and mentally, it is freeing, but also draining and hard!

In the end, we had 4 bins that we left in my parent's basement. The bins had things like keepsakes and holiday decorations we didn't want to get rid of. And this is 100% OK to keep a few bins with these kinds of things in them.

Think you are done?? Yes and no!

Ongoing Downsizing

Talk to anyone on the road, and they will tell you this purging process happens multiple times a year while you are in the RV. It is crazy how you can still accumulate things. The problem in an RV is you run out of places to put things, so nothing ends up hidden, and instead, it starts encroaching on your living space. This prompts you to go through everything again and get rid of things way sooner than you would if you had a house and multiple closets, attic and basement storage.

When we downsized from our 39-foot motorhome down to the 23-foot class C, we had to go through this process again. You'd think we would be pros at this! Not quite. We ended up paying like $200 to send a big box of things and books back to Craig's parents that we didn't think we weren't ready to get rid of.

We went back to his parent's house a few months later and after going through everything, we ended up getting rid of most of it anyway! Maybe we will learn one day.

Don't get me wrong, we still go to Target for toothpaste and leave with $100 worth of things in the cart. But now we have a whole different perspective. We walk in those stores and stop to ask ourselves, do we really need this? Do we have room for it? It can sometimes be overwhelming since those stores are so good at making you think you absolutely need it! That's when I start getting into the flight mode of I need to get out of this store!!

Now our kids have not chosen to live minimally. We are making them do this. For that reason we try to keep things in their life that allows them to see both sides. Each month we give them $20 that they can use to go out and buy whatever they want. If they want to buy a new toy or a game on their tablet, whatever it might be, they can.

Some of the things they buy they may use for a week or a month, and then we donate it or give it to someone else. We look at those things like experiences. When you go to do a ropes course, you may spend $30 on that 1-hour experience. How is that different from buying a toy that you may play with for a couple of hours or weeks and then pass it on?

The kids are really amazing with all of this and tend to let go of things a lot quicker than Craig and I. Over the years, we have also left a few things back at their grandparent's house. Things like a dirt bike, nerf guns, ride-on toys. Things we didn't have room for or things they wanted to keep nice and clean (Carson is all about taking care of his things, and he knows at his grandparents it will stay nice, clean and organized). This is also fun when we go back. It's like they have brand new toys to play with!

We have met families on the road who got a storage unit before they left, and ended up regretting it since they had to put time into going back to go through all of that stuff a year later and got rid of most of it anyway!

If you have plans to buy a new house in a year or settle down in the near future, you may want to keep all of your furniture, especially if it is nice stuff. But that means just furniture - not all the other stuff!

What About Holiday Decorations?

We have a few things for each holiday that we have kept to use year after year, but for the most part, we buy new things every year to decorate and then donate them when we are done. Easy and simple. Plus, it is fun to go to the store to pick out new decorations every year.

Overall, I think possessions really take hold of you and your mental focus. It is very freeing to be able to downsize just what you need. It is also challenging and hard and when you add the kids and their emotions into the mix, it can get even harder.

But I am telling you, once you get going and you do it, it gets easier to keep doing it. And you will do it again. You would be amazed at how much you can accumulate in a small space! Almost every other RVer we talk to tells us that they do a purge about every 3 months, if not more.

When you are in such a small space, everything is in front of you, so you see it all the time and want it gone or want more space, so your rig doesn't feel as cramped. Every time we do a purge, it feels so good to go through and get everything back down to just what we need!

We hope that by living this way and showing this to our kids, we teach them not to be attached to possessions. But instead, live a life of freedom from things and a focus on exploring, adventure and each other!

So what do you really need to keep?

RV Kitchen Accessories

It is all about minimizing. Unfortunately, a lot of big kitchen appliances probably aren't going to work. Instead, we focused on things we were going to use day in and day out. If we didn't use it in a month, it was gone.

Cast Iron Skillet

We prefer a cast iron one (12 inch Lodge Cast-Iron Skillet) since cooking in cast iron is very healthy. This is totally your own preference. Yes, they take some getting used to (you can't wash them with soap, and you should dry them right away, plus things stick to them, so clean them quickly – or boil a little water to help remove the food). But we feel the health benefits are worth it.

Cast Iron Dutch Oven Pot

This is the only pot we have for cooking. Yes, sometimes it is larger than what we need, but it always works for what we are trying to do. Mac and cheese, spaghetti, corn on the cob, hot dogs, all work in the Lodge Cast Iron Dutch Oven with dual handles. Just be aware these pots and pans are heavy!

Countertop Griddle

Have to have this for pancakes and grilled cheese!

9X13 Glass Baking Dish

You have to have something to make cookie bars and cake in, right?! The 9X13 Glass Baking Dish is perfect for that. *TIP – make sure the propane oven or convection microwave you have in your RV can fit a pan this size.* If not, you may need an 8X8 size pan. Also, if you plan on taking a lot of meals or cookie bars to places, you may want to get a dish that comes with a cover.

9 X 13 Small Cookie Pan

I used to bake all the time, so this felt like a necessity to me. I have used it a few times, so I am glad I had it. Again measure the size of the oven or convection microwave to see what size will fit. For us, the 9 X 13 pan fits great.

Toaster

We have room for a toaster, so we kept one, plus I splurged and got one that matched the color scheme of the RV. After a few times moving, I quickly learned it was easier to put it away in a drawer. I still love the way it matches our colors any time we bring out the toaster. If you like toast, find space for it. You will be glad you did.

Donut Maker

Necessities, remember! We actually use our Babycakes Nonstick Coated Donut Maker quite a bit and are happy we have it. If it isn't donuts for you but something else you know you make more than once a month and need a special appliance, bring it with you. P.S. We know this is non-stick, but hey, once they make a cast iron donut maker like this, we will be all over it!

Coffee Pot/Espresso Maker

This lifestyle is all about having more time. So we make complicated coffee – but it is good! And we have been delighted with our Moka Express Espresso Maker – I actually prefer our coffee to Starbucks now!

A regular coffee maker would work too. Or if tea is your thing, then an electric kettle would be the route to go.

Dishes

We have 1 plate for each person. We travel with glass plates and have had no issues. Nothing goes between them when we travel, and they have been fine. We have 8-inch size square plates, and they work great.

Bowls

We have 1 glass bowl per person. Again, all we need.

Glasses

We use mason jars for all of our glasses. We have a few in each size (8 ounces, 12 ounces, 32 ounces). We use them quite a lot, so I would highly recommend them and no issues on travel days. However, with these, we sometimes put a kitchen towel in-between them since they can clatter and make noise. It can be hard to find individual ones, so you may want to find someone else to split a set with. The only place I have found them individually is at Party City.

We also have some stainless steel cups that work great.

Coffee cups

We have 2, one for Craig and one for me, and that is it. If one breaks, we buy another one or use a mason jar for a while. Those things are darn useful! Craig got me one for my birthday from Starbucks that says Wisconsin on it – representing the hometown. Craig bought one for himself down in the Florida Keys – to remind us of our time there.

Cutting boards

Another thing you will want to have. Even just a small one or one that can go over your sink.

Blender

We have a blender since we make smoothies almost every morning. We got a Vitamix, and we love it!

Silver Ware

1 knife, 1 fork, and 1 spoon for everyone. You just wash them when you are done.

Cutting Knives

A nice set of knives with covers on them is useful. I really like the covers since it makes it easy to bring them with us when we go on hikes or are gone for the day and want to pack a lunch. We got ours at Costco.

Essential oil diffuser

RVs can get stinky. Small space, black tanks, pets . . . an oil diffuser really helps to make the RV smell nice, and there are health benefits to the oils!

Mixing Bowl

One large mixing bowl. For mixing doughnut and pancake mix! Again check the size of your rig and where you will be storing your bowl to see how big you can go. We also use this bowl for popcorn on movie nights.

Ziploc Containers

These come in really handy on travel days. But we are trying to move away from plastic and use reusable containers or mason jars. For now, Ziploc containers work great.

Hydro Flask Water Bottles

Everyone has their own Hydro Flask water bottle, and this is what we mainly use for drinking throughout the day, on hikes and in the car. We basically take them everywhere we go. We use an Igloo Cooler bag that we use to carry all 6 of them around.

Berkey Filter

Our Berkey filter is essential for nice fresh water no matter where we are. Did you know water tastes different depending on where you are in the country? Seriously! But with a Berkey, it always tastes fresh and clean. We currently have the smaller travel size so it fits under our cabinets. With 6 people we fill it multiple times a day but it works. In the past we have had the Big Berkey as well.

Utensils

Your basics. 1 spatula, 1 can opener, 1 wine bottle opener, 1 bottle opener, 1 large plastic spoon, 1 coffee grinder (since we make coffee from beans).

Oven Gloves

Gotta have the 'Ove Glove' for cooking.

Kitchen Towels

Three should be plenty.

Instant pot

A lot of RVers will tell you this is a must. We got one and didn't use it that much. I guess it depends on what you normally cook. If you usually use a crockpot, make a lot of rice or do a lot of meat the Instant Pot may be a good fit for you. Same thing with a crockpot. It just isn't how we cook.

Propane Grill

We don't cook outside much at all. We used to romanticize being in an RV and cooking outside every night. The reality is it is a lot of work to bring everything outside to cook! And the RV kitchen is so accessible and easy to use.

We eat outside at the picnic table from time to time but normally will cook all our food inside and then bring it outside. But when we do get around to wanting to grill, the Coleman Classic Propane Stove is great! Plus, our cast iron griddle fits perfectly on it. Just don't forget the propane! It is the worst when you get all set up and then realize you are out of propane.

Tension Rods For The Fridge

Things move around in the fridge when you are driving. We purchased tension rods for the fridge, and they have been helpful.

Sink Strainer

This inexpensive little gadget can save you from having a gray tank clogged up with coffee grinds or seeds. Get a sink strainer.

Colander

Great for straining food. A collapsible one is even better and is a great space saver!

You can find links to the products we mention above on our site at: https://www.crazyfamilyadventure.com/rv-kitchen-accessories/

RV Kitchen Tips:

- Plan your meals ahead of time, so you don't overbuy. This is annoying when you have to get your list together. But really nice when you have limited space.
- The fridge and freezer are not that big, so buy smaller size items when you can. But don't over-stress. Most RV fridges

can easily fit a gallon of milk.

- Don't buy everything you need for a whole 2 or 3-week trip. You can easily stop at the grocery store with your rig.
- If you are going to buy frozen pizza, check your oven size and your freezer size, and if you have to just take the pizza out of the box to store in the freezer. It is a great space-saving trick.

Your rig will most likely have either a propane stove or a convection microwave for an oven.

- Propane stove – don't be afraid of it. They really do a great job cooking your food!
- Convection Microwave – As long as you preheat it before using it, it will work out great. I also recommend if you are cooking 2 pizzas (they won't fit in there together), then when one pizza is done, let the fan run to cool it down and then preheat again before cooking the next one. I don't know why but this really made a big difference for the second pizza.

If you preheat, the cooking time is normally pretty close to what the box says. However, there will be times you have to cook a little more.

Also, the convection microwave can act as a storage space too.

Above all, remember you need the basics, and it is good to simplify but if there is something that you really enjoy, then bring it with you (the donut maker in our case). Just try to limit what those things are to 1 or 2 things. And guess what? If you end up wishing you had something with you – you can always stop at the store to buy one. More often than not, you will realize you didn't really need it anyway.

Clothes

I can't believe how many clothes I used to have in our old house. I had 2 closets full! Now I have one bin full and a few hangers, and that is it.

It really is crazy, but I have learned that I really only wear a small number of clothes. Granted, if I had to go to work every day or dress nice, I would probably need more, but that is one of the many benefits of this lifestyle. I can wear yoga pants or workout clothes every day!

For the kids, I have found that having a bin full of campground play clothes works great. I don't care if this stuff gets messy or ruined. Then I have a collection of 2 to 3 outfits that are nice clothes that they only wear when going out to eat, to a museum, exploring, etc.

It truly is amazing how little clothes you really do need to have. I should add we and our kids will wear the same clothes for a couple of days in a row. Why not?! Less laundry and way are easier to maintain!

Chapter 8

Things You Need

In this chapter we share a collection of things we think you will need and want in your RV.

Internet

Oh, the Internet . . . I think it is a good thing that we left our house right after we got rid of cable and moved to internet TV watching. And before our kids started wanting to stream on their iPads. Reason being, we didn't know what we were missing by not having reliable internet all the time to handle all that bandwidth!

If you need the internet to run your business, DON'T rely on campground wifi. SERIOUSLY. It rarely works, and if it does you usually have to be at the clubhouse or a designated area for it to really work.

Instead, we recommend getting your own hotspot. If you always need a connection and don't want to stress about having to drive to a location (hello, Starbucks), then you may want to get a Verizon and an AT&T plan. Plus a booster never hurts.

I will say we have made running multiple online businesses work with just a Verizon hotspot, but there have been campgrounds and locations where it was a total nightmare and a booster or AT&T would have really helped.

We are by no means experts on this and recommend that you check out RV Mobile Internet for up-to- date, helpful information on the internet and best options. You can find it here: https://www.rvmobileinternet.com/

Memberships

There are a decent amount of RV memberships sites out there. Here are the ones we recommend:

Fulltime Families

Fulltime Families or FTF is all about families traveling full-time in their RV. Lots of great resources and rallies! If you are on the road full time and you are interested in finding community this is a great way to do it. They do have a free membership, but if you buy a membership you get access to their niche specific groups built around traveling locations, interests, etc. There are also discount benefits you get for joining and you have access to their rallies and events.

Thousand Trails

Great for inexpensive camping (once you buy the membership), and for meeting other full-time traveling families. The campgrounds themselves are normally just OK. They tend to be further out from attractions and a lot of them are somewhat run down.

Still, they usually have pools, decent-sized sites and are a great way to meet other full-time traveling families.

Be aware that quite a few are not in good cell signal areas. It is always worth it to call and ask or to check out one of the many Thousand Trails groups or Fulltime Families Thousand Trails groups on Facebook to learn more about connectivity at the campgrounds.

We have a love/hate relationship with Thousand Trails campgrounds. We love all the people we meet there, the pools and the fun amenities a lot of them have. And, it is so easy to make and change reservations online. We don't love most of the locations and the cell signal issues. If you are looking for a 5 star resort campground, these usually are not what you want.

Passport America

This provides great discounts on campgrounds (usually for one to two nights, but sometimes more). If you are someone who is all about looking for deals, this would be a great membership to have. Oftentimes, the deals are only for during the week, in the off season, or just a few nights. But it can make a difference in your campground expenses for the month.

Good Sam

When you RV full time you should have Good Sam. It is nice for 10% discounts at a lot of campgrounds plus discounts on RV supplies at Camping World.

Good Sam Roadside Assistance

The roadside assistance was very helpful when our tire blew as we were driving down the road! It's made for RVers so they understand the situation you are in. It was great to be able to call one number and have them take care of finding someone to come out and help us with a blown tire on the side of the highway.

This is a good resource to have for peace of mind knowing you have someone to call that understands RV travel if you have a breakdown.

Good Sam offers a variety of other services. We have not taken advantage of any of the additional ones, but they are all worth looking into before you get started.

Harvest Host

This provides great opportunities to stay for free at wineries, breweries, golf courses, museums, farms, etc! We LOVE Harvest Host. You can park your rig at a winery and go in for a tasting. If you are lucky, you may be there when they have live music going on, and then can walk right back to your home on wheels. YES!!

They also offer Golf Course stays now. My husband loves that we can park in a golf course parking lot and he can go and hit balls at night and get up in the morning and head out for a round of golf. The golf courses usually have a restaurant or bar, so it is nice to go grab a bite to eat or a drink while you are staying there, too.

The museum and farm stays are also really unique ways to spend the night. We stayed at an Alpaca Farm in Montana and it was awesome! We have also stayed in museum parking lots - one was even attached to an indoor water park!

They also have a great app!

Boondockers Welcome

Boondockers Welcome is a great way to find unique stays on people's property around the US! These are homes or properties of people who love RVers and are interested in meeting new people. We stayed with an awesome couple who had ice cream waiting for us when we got there, and took the kids out on an ATV the next day.

We have heard from others who have had the same kind of experiences where the host took them out on their boat or to walk around their farm to feed the animals. If you are staying with kids, just be sure to let the owners know to make sure that is OK.

Reciprocal Museum Membership

A great one for deals on science museums, natural history museums, children's museums and more! This membership paid for itself over and over again. Basically, 2 visits to a museum with our family of 6 and the cost of the reciprocal membership was paid.

National Park Pass

Another MUST-have pass if you are hitting the road. The National Park Pass is $80 for the year and gets you into all the National Parks (done per vehicle – includes your towed car IF it is connected to your rig when you pull in). It gets you into 2,000 federal recreation sites including

National Forests, National Wildlife Refuges and more!

There are a lot of options out there, but these are the main ones that we have used over the years.

RV Blogs/Podcasts/YouTube Channels

There are a ton of great RV blogs, Instagram channels and YouTube channels you can check out to get different perspectives on full-time RV travel with kids. They are also great platforms for helping to figure out where to go and where to stay when you get somewhere.

You can search Instagram by hashtags like #fulltimervfamily or #fulltimefamilies. For blogs you can search RV Family Blogs to get a list of great blogs to follow. For YouTube search full-time RV families. There is a lot of content out there!

Here are a few of our favorites:

Heath and Alyssa

Website: https://heathandalyssa.com/

Heath and Alyssa Padgett started full-time RVing right around the time we did. They also run the RV Entrepreneur Summit which is amazing! And the RV Entrepreneur Podcast. All of these resources have been instrumental to us on the road.

RV Mobile Internet

Website: https://www.rvmobileinternet.com

RV Mobile Internet is Craig's go to when we are trying to figure out anything internet related for the RV. They have great content on their Facebook page and an awesome membership where you can stay up to date on everything RV internet related.

Less Junk More Journey

YouTube: https://www.youtube.com/c/LessJunkMoreJourney

Nathan and Marissa do an amazing job producing content on their YouTube channel. It is an inspiring and fun way to learn more about this lifestyle.

Keep Your Daydream

YouTube: https://www.youtube.com/c/KeepYourDaydreamTv/

This is another great YouTube channel that has tons of great information about getting on the road and things to do at places you visit. Marc and Tricia know how to put together beautiful and helpful videos.

RV Entrepreneur Podcast

I mentioned this above but want to mention it again. The RV Entrepreneur podcast is awesome if you want to learn different ways to be an RV entrepreneur!

RV Upgrades

We also wanted to share our favorite RV upgrades. Not all of these are necessary for living full time in an RV with kids, but a lot of them are really nice to have!

Solar

We really like to boondock, so the ability to harness free solar power from the sun is amazing. The word "solar" encompasses many different components to an overall system. This includes solar panels (either on the roof or portable), a solar charge controller to regulate the amount of electricity going into the batteries, an inverter to invert the 12 volt power stored in the batteries to 120 volts as well as the batteries, which I'll talk more about next.

Getting a quality system installed on your rig to meet your needs is an investment that can pay off big time. We worked with Future Solutions for a fantastic setup that allows us to be off grid for as long as we want.

In the past, we have also had homemade solar setups - where we purchased everything ourselves and Craig installed it all. This was not a fancy setup and didn't run to our outlets but instead, we just had an extension cord and a power strip. We also didn't upgrade to lithium but just had 6 volt golf cart batteries. It was by no means as nice as what we have now. But it worked and we boondocked for weeks in Baja, Utah and a few other places with this setup. Plus it cost about a quarter of what the setup we have now cost.

Batteries

RV's usually come with a single 12-volt battery. This is fine to keep the lights on for a while and run the electrical part of a gas fridge, but if you're looking to camp off grid, adding more battery capacity or even a different type of battery is one of the best RV mods you can do.

There are many different options out there like lead acid, AGM and more recently, lithium. Having a higher capacity battery bank allows you to stay unplugged longer and really get out to some epic spots.

We currently have the Battle Born GC3's and we are really liking them!

Generator

If solar isn't an option, then having an on-board or portable generator is a great upgrade for dry camping. We have a Honda 2000 watt generator that is a great alternative for the solar when it's overcast for a few days.

Suspension

If you want to get out to epic spots, you need to be sure your rig can handle the rugged terrain it has to go through to get there. We worked with MORryde to have their Independent Suspension package installed on our Montana High Country 5th wheel.

Their Independent Suspension system allows each wheel to move independently of any other wheel. Usually each wheel is tied to another wheel, either by being on the same axle or by the leaf spring suspension. The benefit is that this allows the wheels to absorb a ton of road shock without moving the house part of the RV which keeps your valuables safe and stable. It also helps a ton with towing as you can't even feel the trailer behind you.

Disc Brakes

Another upgrade MORryde offers, one that usually goes hand-in-hand with Independent Suspension, is upgrading to disc brakes. Trailers and 5th wheels usually come with electric brakes which just don't have the braking power that hydraulic disc brakes do. One of Craig's main concerns with pulling a fully loaded, heavy trailer, especially down mountain grades is the ability to stop it. With disc brakes, this is a non-concern as they offer a 40% shorter stopping distance and reduce heat build up.

Tires

Tires are very easy to overlook when it comes to an RV or trailer. The only time they're looked at is when you have a blow out, which is too late. There are many tire brands out there that are known to have blowouts, which is why upgrading tires is a great peace of mind upgrade.

We upgraded from Load Range F 12-ply tires to Sailun S637 Load Range G 14-ply tires. The difference is substantial. The tires are much more heavy duty and can handle the weight of our rig much better.

Tire Pressure Monitor System

Most modern cars have a TPMS built right in, so we're used to knowing tire pressures in our car and even get notified when they get low. Knowing this information for a trailer is crucial and can be the difference in getting off safely to the side of the road when you have tire problems.

We use the EEZTire TPMS, which is easy to install, easy to use and easy to read. Definitely recommend this.

Trailer Hitch

If you're towing a travel trailer, then the hitch is a great upgrade. We've used a Propride 3P Hitch in the past and it made a world of difference. Again, safety and comfort are your main priorities when towing a trailer and when we were towing our 30′ Jayco trailer, it was swaying all over the road to the point that even short easy drives were white-knuckle ones. No fun. After upgrading to the ProPride 3P, the trailer stayed inline and we had no problems with sway.

Cargo Tray

We all carry stuff in our RV, sometimes too much stuff. This can mean really using every inch of storage space which can make it hard to access some of the things in the storage bays. We upgraded to a very nice MORryde cargo tray that allows us to pull out the tray and access all the stuff that is usually stuck in the middle.

Cell Booster

Being out in the wilderness is great, but we still have to work and that requires a cell signal. Having a cell booster on our rig definitely helps improve a poor signal.

Another option that is less expensive, but requires a certain connection to your hotspot is this Netgear Antenna. We use this one quite often, and it really helps.

Tank Heaters

We love the mountains and that usually means colder temperatures. We have tank heaters for our fresh, grey and black tanks which are turned on by a switch near our control panel and which supplies electrically created heat to the tanks so they don't freeze. Very handy, especially when overnight lows get down below freezing.

RV Steps

A must-do upgrade is MORryde's StepAbove Steps. If you've ever gone in or out of a set of fold-out trailer steps, you know how unstable they feel, not to mention the feeling inside of the entire RV tipping over. The StepAbove steps solve that problem with a set of steps that extend to the ground to make them rock solid. They also have several add-on components to the steps including a strut assist lift that makes lifting the steps very easy, a handrail that connects to the steps for extra stability, a storage box that goes in the space the previous fold-out steps went as well as motion-activated lights that install under each step making going in and out much safer and easier.

Stabilizers

Speaking of feeling like the RV is tipping over, upgrading the stabilizers on a trailer is a must. Having 4 kids that like to run around and wrestle, it constantly felt like we were a ship out on the ocean.

Our rig came with a 4 point leveling/stabilizing system. We upgraded our 5th wheel landing gear with a MORryde X-brace 5th wheel stabilizer that locks it in from side to side motion.

Also, we added MORryde's Hitch Mount Stabilizer to the rear 2″ hitch receiver on our 5th wheel that really locks us in. It makes a world of difference compared to not having these upgrades. Both of these products are easy to install and can remain on your rig even when you're traveling.

We also use a set of X-Chock wheel stabilizers to take out any wheel play that may happen.

Fantastic Fans with Vent Covers

Air flow is a great thing when you're in the great outdoors. RV's can have some funky smells in them, so keeping fresh air flowing is a must. Upgrading the ceiling fans is a great way to do that. We have a couple of Fan-Tastic fans that really maximize air flow keeping the RV fresh. We also have vent covers for these fans so they can operate or remain open when we are driving or if it's raining.

Shower Head

Another easy upgrade which provides better water pressure in the shower as well as conserving water, is changing the shower head. We've used Oxygenics in the past and it's an easy and cheap upgrade that's worth it.

RV Apps

Here are a few of the top RV Apps that are out there.

RV Trip Wizard

RV Trip Wizard is a web tool and an app (when purchasing the membership you also get the RV Life App!). It is a favorite utility of mine and truly makes the road trip planning process seamless.

This awesome program allows you to customize your route however you see fit. It gives you the option to add in truck stops, restaurants, and attractions along the way, and provides detailed information on hundreds of campgrounds. It also allows you to narrow your campground search based on the memberships you have, meaning you can specify that you only want to see Good Sam parks or Thousand Trails parks.

I love that the program uses the information I put in to tally up the total cost of my trip, and that my route can be exported to a GPS or Google Maps. You can combine RV Trip Wizard with the RV Life App (included in your membership) which is like having an RV GPS in your pocket!

The Dyrt

This free app provides information on thousands of campsites all across the United States. From boondocking locations to full-fledged RV resorts, The Dyrt gives users a chance to read reviews written by fellow campers and leave reviews of their own.

Additionally, you can request to reserve a site from the app, making it a cinch to find camping spots.

They have a free version or a paid version: The Dyrt PRO camping app offers trip planning (which is awesome!), offline app access (such a great feature), downloadable maps, gear discounts and camping discounts at hundreds of campgrounds.

Allstays

If you have an iPhone or iPad, another fabulous option for finding places to stay is the Allstaysapp. Ten bucks is what you'll pay to use this popular camping app, and it's worth every penny.

Read reviews from various locations and find the perfect campgrounds, dump stations, rest stops, and more. Filter stops by amenities, and quickly check for road conditions and emergencies. Best of all, you can search while offline, meaning you can even use this app in remote locations!

RV Parky

Built by a full-time RVer with the help of the RV community, RV Parky claims to be home of the most complete collection of RV campgrounds out there. The app provides user reviews and photos, helping make your trip planning a bit easier.

This RV app doesn't do as much as the ones mentioned above, but we love the simplicity of it!

Hipcamp

Hipcamp is something like Airbnb except for campers. It allows people with spare land to rent their space to campers, meaning a whole new world of camping opportunities for you.

The Hipcamp app allows users to easily search for and reserve Hipcamp campsites. You can read reviews, narrow your search by certain criteria, and even access certain information offline.

Campendium

The final campground finder app on our list is the Apple-exclusive Campendium app. We use this app often, especially when looking for boondocking sites across North America.

The free app provides camper-written reviews of thousands of campsites, including many we haven't found on any other review website. Additionally, Campendium provides cell reception information, something many full-time RVers need to have.

Google Maps

Quite possibly the most-used navigation app out there, Google Maps is our go-to navigation app. We love that it gives multiple route options, and we can choose to avoid tolls. We also appreciate the street view option, which allows us to check out certain roads and parking lots to make sure they will work for our rig.

Mountain Directory

The final route planning tool that we recommend is the *Mountain Directory. This also isn't truly an app, but rather a set of two ebooks. Mountain Directory West costs $17, while Mountain Directory East costs $15.*

The books provide invaluable information on mountains passes and steep grades, helping you plan the safest travel route possible. Considering Google Maps doesn't provide this information, we find this tool quite useful.

Weather Apps for Planning Travels

Weather apps can help you see what the weather will be like wherever you plan to travel. This allows you to route around a location if the weather looks bad, or at least be prepared for any storms or extreme temperatures that may come your way.

These apps are also great because they will alert you of severe weather, giving you a chance to take shelter if necessary.

Accuweather

Accuweather is one of the most accurate weather apps out there, making planning that much easier. It provides information not usually found in weather apps, such as UV index and the "RealFeel". We also love that it provides a live weather radar and real-time alerts, meaning we are always aware when severe weather is headed our way while out in our RV.

The Weather Channel

Another fantastic option is The Weather Channel's app. This app also provides weather alerts and a live radar, keeping you up-to-date in severe weather. One of the things we love most about this app is the fact that it provides Allergy Insights, meaning we know when to stay indoors to avoid allergy attacks.

Apps for Finding Activities

Of course, you're going to want to find things to do during your RV travels. Luckily, the United States is chock-full of awesome sights to see and things to experience.

We like using the apps below to fill out our itinerary. Whether you're hoping to take a break along your route or want to fill your days once you arrive at your destination, the RV apps listed can help you find the perfect options for your family.

Roadtrippers

Roadtrippers is a lot like RV Trip Wizard, but with some features missing. We tend to use it to find fun things to do and see along our route. The app allows you to search along your route and has thousands of attractions saved, meaning you won't miss any of the awesome sights as you travel.

AllTrails

Most RVers do some amount of hiking as they travel. After all, hiking is one of the best ways to see the national park trails and the state parks out there.

If you need a way to find the best hiking trails in the United States, AllTrails is the app for you. This app allows you to search for trails in a certain area and provides descriptions, reviews, and even difficulty ratings for each trail. They also offer offline maps so you can download the map/trail to have when you are hiking out of range!

National Parks Trail Guide

Offering complete information on the hiking trails in many of the most popular United States national parks, the National Park Trail Guide is a fantastic app. This app offers maps and details to help you choose and navigate trails, and it even works offline, meaning it can be used in those more remote national parks locations.

Apps to Use While Driving

Sanidumps RV Dump Station Locator

To find dump stations, I recommend using the Sanidumps RV Dump Station Locator app. This app makes finding nearby dump stations a cinch. Unfortunately, it's only available on the Google Play Store, meaning Apple users will need to use their website.

RV Dump Stations

For Apple users, I recommend the RV Dump Stations app. Unlike the Sanidumps app, this one costs a bit of money ($1 to be exact). However, we find that it is money well spent, as we can almost always find state parks, campgrounds, or truck stops that will allow us to get rid of our waste water after some time spent boondocking.

GasBuddy

Motorhomes tend to be gas guzzlers, and trucks pulling trailers use their fair share of fuel. Save money on those countless fill-ups by using the GasBuddy app to find the closest gas stations and truck stops with the cheapest fuel prices.

FreeZone Wifi

One of the things RVers are always looking for is a decent internet connection. FreeZone Wifi offers the perfect solution by finding and connecting users to free wifi networks in the surrounding area using crowdsourced data. While this app is only available on Android devices, there are other apps such as WiFi Map for Apple devices that do the same thing.

Audible

One of our favorite forms of entertainment during our RV travels is audiobooks. Get access to thousands of audiobooks and find something for everyone by downloading the Audible app. You will need to pay for the books you listen to, but monthly subscriptions make this easy and painless.

Great Apps for in the Campground

Think you won't need RV apps anymore once you arrive at your campground of choice? Think again! There is one app we find ourselves using in campgrounds and RV parks often, and we think you'll love it just as much as we do.

Speedtest

As mentioned before, RVers are always looking for the fastest internet connection possible. Even those who have a mobile hotspot may have difficulty getting a good connection, especially in state parks and national park campgrounds which can be very remote. This is where Speedtest comes into play.

Speedtest is a handy app that tests the speed of your internet connection. You can use this to choose the campsite with the best connection in any given campground.

That should be enough to get you started. The reality is we don't use all of these all of the time. But we have used all of them at some point! As you get on the road and figure out your travel and planning style you will be able to narrow it down to which ones you use consistently.

Here is a post with links to each app: https://www.crazyfamilyadventure.com/rv-apps/

Moving on to more things that you need, the next chapter gets into Health Insurance and what it is like on the road when someone needs to go to the doctor or an emergency happens.

Chapter 9

Health Insurance

One of the biggest challenges of RVing full-time is finding health insurance for full-time RVers. While some people can acquire insurance through remote-jobs, many people are left to find their own health insurance.

Because paying full price for traditional insurance is so expensive, many wanderers go without insurance entirely. Not only is this risky, but it also comes with tax penalties. Are you willing to live with that risk or those penalties? Some would have you believe you'll have to throw away those RV dreams and stick with a normal, boring 9–5 job to hold onto affordable healthcare coverage.

Fortunately—and despite popular belief—going without insurance, paying an arm and a leg for a private policy, or staying stationary aren't the only options available to you. We will discuss other health insurance options so you can feel confident in your healthcare coverage before hitting the road. We will also share our experience on the road of broken bones and emergencies. With kids, there is always a chance something could happen.

Healthcare Marketplace

The first option is to check out the Healthcare Marketplace. This is a government-run program created by the Affordable Care Act. It offers a subsidy to families who fall under certain income guidelines. This subsidy can be applied to the premium of a health insurance plan listed on the site.

With plans from such well-known companies as Blue Cross, you can feel good about your coverage, and the subsidy helps make these plans affordable.

The Healthcare Marketplace is where we recommend starting your search for affordable healthcare, but if this option doesn't work for you, the options below can help.

This is what we have been using since we became full-time entrepreneurs over 5 years ago. Unfortunately, the plans have changed over the years, and now the only coverage you can get is within the state you live in. Meaning everything out of state is out-of-network.

If you look closely through the plans, you can find plans that offer Emergency room coverage throughout all of the US. In some cases, the ER visit is covered 100% after your deductible is met. In others, it is a co-insurance option. The good thing is you are covered for emergency visits out of state. NOT ALL PLANS HAVE THIS, SO LOOK CLOSELY AND CALL TO CONFIRM.

This was extremely helpful for us this year when our son broke his ankle when we were in Idaho. We are from Wisconsin, so we were pretty far out of network! We explained the situation to the ER doctor. They did x-rays and determined it was broken and not just broken but in the ER doctor's words - broken really bad . . .

They called in an orthopedic specialist, and we explained our situation to him as well. In these cases, you do have to be vocal and upfront about your situation. His goal was to set the ankle and let the swelling go down. Then he recommended having surgery on it in about a week when the swelling was down.

In this case, the plan was to get the ankle set, and we would head back to Wisconsin for the surgery.

He attempted to set it in the ER, and he couldn't even move it. The swelling was that bad. He said we couldn't leave with it like this, so he needed emergency surgery to fix the ankle ASAP.

He had surgery that night, and everything didn't wrap up until about 11:30 pm, so they had us stay overnight in the hospital. He ended up with 2 plates and 11 screws - yes, it was bad . . .

Throughout this process, I told everyone I talked to that we had to be sure this was marked as emergency room coverage. I eventually talked to the caseworker and shared that as well.

The next day we headed home. I knew our insurance wouldn't cover the follow-up appointments, and we would be paying a couple of hundred dollars out of pocket for all of those. But the main surgery was what I was concerned about.

We called our Insurance, and they confirmed that it would cover it. We got our bills, and they ended up being over $30,000!!!! Say what?! I called the insurance company, and they had to go through an appeals process to deal with the balanced billing and talk to the hospital to come to an agreement.

The insurance company assured me we would only have to pay our son's deductible - which is $6700. But we knew that when we signed up.

Needless to say, everything would have been much better in-network. But even being out of network, it was manageable, and we were able to get done what needed to be done.

We did sign up for the same plan for 2021 as he will have to have surgery in September to get the plates and screws removed - which we plan to do in Wisconsin. The other insurance plans we looked at would not cover this surgery since it was pre-existing. So it was nice that we had this plan we could stay with.

There is no perfect solution in our eyes, and there won't be until we have Universal Healthcare (which I know won't be perfect, but it will at least ensure we have coverage for everything everywhere we go.) In the meantime, everyone needs to pick the best plan that works for them, their family, and their needs.

Below are other options you can look at:

Fixed-Benefit Insurance

A fixed-benefit insurance plan is different from traditional insurance in that users pay a fixed rate for a preselected set of benefits. Unfortunately, this type of insurance won't cover all medical expenses, meaning it's best used as supplemental coverage. Still, some people in good health feel this type of coverage is enough to keep them safe as they experience full-time RV living.

If you choose to use only a fixed benefit plan, you might consider setting up a health savings account (HSA). Not only will this ensure you have the funds to cover medical emergencies that aren't covered by your fixed-benefit insurance plan, but the money put into these accounts is tax-deductible, too.

United Healthcare is one insurance company that offers fixed-benefit health insurance plans.

Short-Term Health Insurance

Short-term insurance is a unique type of coverage. As the name implies, this kind of insurance is meant to be used for short periods of time and is usually purchased by those needing coverage between jobs.

The definition of "short term" varies from one provider to the next, but some insurance companies will allow customers to use these plans for up to three years. Obviously, this won't cover you forever if you plan to stay on the road for the long term, but it is enough to allow you to hit the road and settle into the nomad life before solving the health insurance puzzle.

This type of plan is also perfect for those who only want to travel for a short period of time, as it ensures coverage while you travel and until you can settle down and find another job with benefits.

It is important to note that short-term insurance offers only limited coverage. Therefore, it isn't ideal for those who need to visit the doctor often, but can work for those who only need coverage for urgent care visits or the emergency room.

RVer Insurance Exchange

While it isn't exactly a type of medical insurance, RVer Insurance Exchange definitely deserves mention. This awesome group of insurance professionals help RVers find insurance plans that work for them and their unique lifestyle choices.

The people at RVer Insurance Exchange consider your income, travel style and medical needs to find a plan that works for you. They shop all of the insurance types above for you, and they offer many customers a free telemedicine option to supplement their coverage. All that said, the best thing this group offers is access to group insurance plans for the self-employed RVers out there.

You see, lower-priced group coverage is not usually available to self-employed individuals, as it requires a group of people and an employer to be a part of the mix. With RVer Insurance Exchange, fellow RVers become a part of your "group," and the company works like an employer, offering you coverage at the low rates you might enjoy when working a job with benefits.

Internet-Based Health Care

In recent months we've seen more and more internet-based healthcare options popping up. These programs allow you to visit a doctor via video chat from the comfort of your own home, often even getting prescriptions called in after the visit is complete.

This option is not actually health insurance but can help your family receive the medical care they need at an affordable price while traveling. Such internet-based medical options are perfect to use as a full-timer who may not regularly visit the same primary care physician. We also appreciate the affordability of this option.

One of our favorite internet-based healthcare options is Teledoc by Careington.

Healthcare-Sharing Ministry Plans

Like internet-based care options, healthcare sharing plans are also not true insurance but are still an option to consider. These plans work by making monthly payments from all participants and pooling this money, using it to pay the medical bills of participants as they come in.

This can work, but there are times when the bills are too high, and payments from participants aren't enough to cover them. In these cases, uninsured participants are left without any help, potentially putting them in a major bind.

Another thing to consider is the fact that these programs tend to be faith-based. Most require that participants hold the same beliefs as the organization, and many require participants to provide a signed letter from their pastor. This means those who aren't religious and those whose beliefs don't align with the available health sharing ministries are excluded from this option.

Hopefully, one of these RV health insurance (or other health coverage) options will work for you and keep your family in good health so you can continue to travel the country and make awesome memories doing so.

Our Experiences and Tips

We have had multiple broken bones, surgeries, and skin infections while being on the road. It is never fun on the road or at home when someone in the family isn't feeling well! As we mentioned above, we have Healthcare.gov, and it has met our needs over the years. The other aspect of this outside of just the insurance piece is how to manage everything when you are constantly on the move!

In Carson's case this year - due to the severity of the break, we stayed in the area where it happened and near his doctor for 7 weeks - until he could get the cast removed and a clear checkup. We had all of the hospital records sent to us, so we would have them with us. This is key! Whenever you visit a doctor or even a dentist on the road, be sure to ask for a copy of all the records, x-rays, doctor notes!

When our younger son broke his arm, we ended up seeing about 3 different doctors throughout the process. It took a lot of phone calls and explaining, but eventually, it all worked out. He had his surgery with one doctor, his follow-up with another, and a different one that removed his cast.

These situations aren't normal for the doctor's office, so it always took a lot to explain our situation and what was going on. Over the years, we have learned that you have to keep pushing and asking and talking until they know what you need and can figure out how to help you.

We have also used the Teledoc services a lot to facetime/video call with a doctor. This was super helpful when we had a skin infection that went through our family. Since we already knew what it was (the first kids that got it went into the doctor), we just needed to talk to the doctor, and they could send in the prescription we needed.

But, there was also confusion with this since they said, well, wait - your last prescription went to Nashville, but now you are saying Minnesota - where exactly are you?! There is always additional explanation needed in these situations.

We have learned that if you can be flexible, don't have to be attached to one doctor, and can be good at really asking and telling them what you need (and not letting up until they get it), you will be good. Would it be easier if you were staying in a house in one place? Heck yeah!!

But it is just one of the extra things you have to do to enjoy this lifestyle. We go back to our hometown at least once a year and do our kids' yearly checkups, dentist appointments, etc.

Don't let the challenges of Health Insurance stop you from traveling! Do your research, talk to people, ask the providers questions (lots of questions) and find something that will work for your family. It may not be ideal or perfect, but you should be able to find something!

On to more things you will need to figure out - how to get mail.

Chapter 10

Getting Mail

Another thing you have to consider before jumping living in an RV? Getting your mail. While many of us don't get a whole lot of snail mail these days (I know we don't), there are still some things you have to receive the old-fashioned way.

When the time comes for you to get something in the mail, how will you do it?

Fortunately, there are several different ways to go about getting mail while RVing. Check out the list below to learn how you can continue to receive your mail as you explore our wonderful country.

Friends and Family

If you have friends or family "back home" who are willing, consider asking them to receive your mail for you. My parents and Craig's have helped us out for years by receiving the bulk of our mail and have even been willing to mail items to us when something important has shown up.

This is, of course, a very budget-friendly RV mail option, and it's the perfect option if you wish to maintain residency in your original state or if you'll only be on the road part-time. That said, it does require that you have friends or family that you trust with anything important that may arrive by mail.

If you choose this route, we recommend that you:

- Have a set location where all mail will be kept until you return for a visit, so nothing is lost.
- Keep tabs on when expected mail will arrive. This is especially key if the mail is urgent, so you can ask for it to be forwarded to you.
- Check-in once in a while to ensure nothing urgent has arrived.
- Always pay for shipping if something needs to be sent your way.
- Offer payment to your loved one for doing this favor for you.

This is the option we have chosen over the years. We started with my parents, and when they went full-time in their RV, we switched to Craig's parents. His Mom now gets all of our mail and will send it to us once in a while.

If we get a check in the mail, she will take a picture of it and send it to us as well - so we can deposit it sooner.

It has worked out well, and we are super thankful that she will do this for us!

Mail Forwarding Services

Another RV mail option that you can use is a mail forwarding service. Several companies offer this kind of service, which allows you to have a permanent street address of your own. Any pieces of mail you receive are sent to this address, where employees sort and hold the mail until you request that it be sent to you.

Many of these RV mail forwarding services offer some pretty cool benefits. I've seen companies that offer mail scanning and give you access to an online account that allows you to view your mail online. Additionally, many of these services will throw out junk mail for you, saving you money on shipping costs when it comes time to have the mail sent to you.

Besides having a mailing address of your own, mail forwarding services are also great because they give you a physical address that can actually be used as a home address for driver licensing and other important documents. On top of that, most of these companies will even walk you through the process of changing your residency, should you wish to change your domicile state, making it as painless as possible.

Not sure where to begin your search for an RV mail forwarding service? I've listed some of the more popular options below to get you started:

- **Escapees RV Club:** Offers residency in Florida or Texas.
- **Good Sam Mail Service** — Offers residency in Florida.
- **St. Brendan's Isle** — Offers residency in Florida.
- **My RV Mail:** Offers residency in Florida.
- **Texas Home Base:** Offers residency in Texas.
- **U.S. Global Mail** — Offers residency in Texas
- **Dakota Post:** Offers residency in South Dakota.
- **Your Best Address:** Offers residency in South Dakota.

Campground Mail

Some campgrounds cater to their full-time RVer guests by allowing them to receive mail and/or packages while they stay. This is an option if you rarely receive mail, but because not all campgrounds offer this perk, I would personally be hesitant to lean on it as my only option for getting mail.

What I do use this awesome campground amenity for is receiving packages. These include Amazon deliveries, packages from loved ones, and of course, the mail that has been collected by our parents.

Before having anything sent to a campground:

- Be sure to call ahead and ask if it's okay.
- Confirm that the campground will receive the type of mail you are having sent (package vs. letter) and will accept it from the carrier you plan to use.
- Ask about any fees, as some RV parks will charge a per-package fee.
- Make sure you know when and where you will be allowed to pick up your mail.
- If you aren't sure you'll be there when your mail arrives, ask if it will be held for you and how long they are willing to hold it.

General Delivery

If your campground won't receive mail for you, another option is to turn to the United States Postal Service. The USPS General Delivery service allows you to receive your mail at the post office directly. Sure, you'll have to drive to the post office to pick it up, but it's better than nothing.

To have General Delivery mail sent, address it as follows:

Name

General Delivery

City, State, Zip Code

Usually, General Delivery mail is held for 10 days at the post office, giving you plenty of time to pick it up. General Delivery mail is not delivered on Sundays or holidays, so take that into account when making plans.

Before leaving home to pick up your mail, be sure you know which specific post office it was sent to (some cities have more than one). You'll also want to ensure you have your driver's license or another form of identification.

P.O. Box

If you are going to be in a location for a longer period of time you may want to open a PO Box at USPS or a local mail service store. This can be cost effective and well worth it if you can easily get mail!

Amazon Hub Lockers

Finally, I must mention Amazon Hub Lockers. We have yet to use these lockers, but we have plenty of friends who swear by them, and they look like a convenient way to receive Amazon packages if your campground doesn't receive them for you.

Amazon Hub Lockers are located in more than 900 cities across the US, meaning you'll often be close to one. The lockers allow users three days to pick up packages, and if you cannot pick them up within this timeframe, your packages are automatically returned for a full refund.

I love that these lockers have long hours, making finding a time to pick them up easy. I also appreciate that you can return items to an Amazon locker if you find you ordered the wrong thing. In fact, after researching these, I think I'll have to give them a try for myself.

Using these 5 great RV mail options, you should be able to receive any letters or packages you need while on the road. Whether you choose to mix and match a variety of services and/or favors, or you prefer to stick with just one, you're sure to find out what works well for you fairly quickly, and soon enough, RV mail will no longer seem like such a challenge.

Like Health Insurance, there isn't an ideal solution. . . but there are solutions that work!

Chapter 11

School

What will school look like while you are traveling full-time in an RV with your kids? Well, it is up to you!

You could decide to choose a traditional route where you follow a curriculum or even do public school online. Or you can decide to go a less traditional route. Or you can put together your own mix of curriculums, national parks, museums, etc.

State Rules

Do take note that every state has their own rules for Homeschooling. Some are super easy where you don't have to do anything. Or you just have to fill out a form once a year. And some are stricter and you actually need to take a formal test at the end of the year. Be sure to check your state's requirements. Texas and Florida are popular domicile states that have pretty easy homeschooling rules. In Texas you don't have to do anything (but always double check this) and in Florida you can sign up under the Umbrella Unschooling and then do whatever you want for homeschooling.

Below we share what we are doing for schooling and have been doing ever since our kids were born. Just a heads up - this isn't your traditional route!

Unschooling

We have been Unschooling since our kids were born. They have never had any formal education. At the time we wrote this post they were 6, 4, 4 and 2. Obviously things have changed, but I wanted to share this part for people with younger kids. My best advice for anyone with younger kids is to just enjoy your kids.

They will learn how to read and they will learn math. But at these younger ages it doesn't need to be formal or structured. If you are tired or the kids just aren't into it - then have a lazy day or week or month. It is OK. They will be OK, it will all be OK!

Here it is - what our Unschooling journey started like on the road:

To understand Radical Unschooling you need to do a lot of research and a lot reading and rereading and thinking and evaluating and re-evaluating. If you are interested in this form of schooling and lifestyle, I would recommend doing a lot of research. Below I will share more about the places we recommend going for information on Unschooling. We are by no means experts at it and still have to pull ourselves back over to the Radical side of it almost every day - but we keep trying - and we are hoping we can continue to learn and grow as parents so we can provide this environment for our kids.

For us this time in our kids' life and our life is all about:

- Building a strong relationship and bond with our kids
- Our kids building a strong relationship and bond with each other
- Exposing our kids to as many opportunities as we can
- Sharing experiences with them that we enjoy and that we think they would enjoy. And them sharing their experiences with us.
- Letting them become the people they are meant to be
- Letting them build their self-confidence and self-awareness by having control of their day

- Enjoying watching them explore, learn, grow, discover, fail, and try again, and just be who they are each and every day
- Having trust in our kids that they will make the right decision and in turn teaching them to trust us.
- Believing that all human beings have an innate need and desire to learn.So here is our typical day:

  - The kids usually wake up between 8am and 9am (no alarm is set).
  - We then snuggle and sit on the couch together and sometimes watch tv or sometimes start playing as we get breakfast ready.
  - After this we will normally head outside where the kids just kind of "tool" around - this means there are no set activities or guidelines - they just have open time to do what they want to do. Sometimes that means they play with their toys, go to the park, play with the sand table or water table, really whatever it is they want to do. We do that for most of the morning.
  - After that we go in to eat lunch and usually watch a movie - this is a good time for everyone to just relax for a little bit - especially if it was hot outside!
  - After that we either go somewhere - the park, the pool, the beach, the zoo, to meet friends, the store, whatever it is we have planned for that day. Or else we just stay around the RV and the kids find things to do. Sometimes that means they get out paper and we do arts and crafts, play with Play Doh, play dress up, play "Mom and Dad", play with the dolls, play on Minecraft, or just play with their toys.

By this time our "school" day is done and Craig is home from work. However, our day doesn't stop there. The kids keep on playing, learning and exploring all the way until they go to bed at night.

No, you did not miss part of it - there is no formal education time throughout our day. We don't do worksheets or tests or lesson plans. We let the day unfold and grab on to any learning opportunities that arise. As we hit the road traveling, we know there will be even more awesome opportunities!

There are a LOT of questions that get asked during the day. About all different kinds of things: what does that word mean? how do you spell that? why does that work that way? where is that from? A couple of examples from today: Are there other planets with humans on them in space? When were the planets made? What does NYC spell? (and many more - those are just the ones I remember.)

If I know the answer I answer it - if I don't, we look it up (Google is awesome!).

We have found if it is a question they are asking - they truly and genuinely want to know the answer. So when they are given an answer they remember it, and it makes sense to them because they learned it when they were intrigued by it.

They are always encouraged to ask questions and to question things - what a great way to learn!

There is learning in every aspect of our day. It seems like when you are going to school that part gets overlooked because everyone has to follow the lesson plan and stay on the same page. Which I know needs to happen in order for a classroom to work. I get that! And I think what schools do for kids that don't have any other options is great!

However, we have the option to provide this amazing opportunity to our kids and we are willing to sacrifice cable tv, the best phones, the best clothes, the best stuff, etc, for that opportunity!

We understand as parents that by going this route we have a huge responsibility to make sure we have an atmosphere that is going to lead to them growing and learning as people and individuals. This includes:

- Having fun toys for them to play with (ropes, sand, water, hammers, markers, crayons, etc.)
- Taking them to cool places (Renaissance Faire, Rock Climbing,

Farms, Beaches, New States and Cities, etc)

- Letting our kids play with and experience all types of toys and things - and not limiting them by age (scissors, knives, paint, Play Doh, computers, etc.)

- Letting them experience situations without us dictating to them what the rules are and how something is supposed to be done - but instead letting them experiment and figure it out on their own or with our help, if they ask for it.

- Trusting our kids and knowing that they understand what is in their best interest. And if we know they aren't ready, instead of saying they can't do it, we do it with them. We work together so they are ready to do it on their own in the near future. (An example of this would be swimming - all of our kids learned how to swim on their own by the time they were 3 - without any formal teaching - because we gave them lots of opportunities to be in the water without water wings on. If they weren't ready to swim on their own, we made sure we were there to help them. But if we felt like they could do it, we stood back and watched and let them try on their own.)

- Strewing - This is an unschooling term which refers to leaving items out that our kids may find interesting and/or taking them to new places to experience new things. (Examples: putting out Magna Tiles, a new picture book, new kinds of food, a whole table of random items, driving a new route to see horses in a field, visiting a farm, going to see waterfalls, etc.)

- If any of the kids take a strong interest in something we really try to help them pursue it to the fullest and allow them as much unlimited time on it as we can! (For example, if they are into Reptiles, we take them to as many reptile shows as we can so they can learn more about them, touch them, and feel them. Even if this means just going to the pet store.)

This style of schooling is a partnership between us and our kids. When they share excitement for something, we all enjoy it together.

Their joy becomes our joy and vice versa! It is so rewarding to experience this with our kids!

Part of our responsibility of being Unschooling Parents is that we have to be present with our kids - as much as possible! This isn't always easy and we have to constantly remind ourselves throughout the day to slow down and focus on our kids and to truly be present in the moment.

We are immersed in our children's life - which is an amazing thing! We are so aware and in tune with what our kids are into and what they like and what they don't like. Since we are with them 24/7, they are also able to see how we as parents react and handle situations and thus are learning how real life works.

One of the challenges of taking this approach is making sure that we are not comparing our kids or our family to other people. We are taking a different approach to schooling so our kids are most likely going to be at a different place than kids that are in school - and this is ok - so there is no need to compare or to make sure our kids are doing what they are supposed to do for this grade or for this age. We strongly feel that they will learn what they need to learn when they are ready to learn it.

We are excited about where we have gotten to and where we are going! Each day we learn so much about ourselves, our kids and our family. And we are excited to see what the future holds!

Unschooling - Kids are 10, 8, 8 and 6

I wrote this post back when the kids were 10, 8, 8 and 6. Further into this chapter I will share more about what Unschooling is like with older kids.

We see all the pictures on Facebook of our friends and family heading back to school every fall. We love seeing the pictures! It is also a time for us to reflect on what we are doing and how our kids don't have back to school pictures.

We have thought about taking a picture of us climbing a mountain or swimming at the beach and posting it as our back to school picture. For us, this time of year is about crowds clearing out, not books, pencils and back to school clothes.

It is a bit of an emotional roller coaster. Craig and I both had great school experiences. We played sports and had a lot of friends. I was Homecoming queen and captain of the soccer team and Craig was Mr. Bradford (winner of our high school talent show). We had a great school experience. Craig and I are high school sweethearts.

We question if it is right not to give our kids that same experience, but always come back to the same conclusion. We are giving our kids the world as their classroom and the freedom to be in charge of their own time. And that is a pretty cool thing.

They run around barefoot with dirty feet, dirt in their nails, stains on their clothes and guess what? We don't care, they don't care, there is no one to care or judge. They find something they love: Minecraft, Legos, animal spotting, swimming, hiking, Nerf guns, whatever it may be, and they can be engrossed in it for hours.

Their day is theirs. What a gift. Yes, we do take them places they don't always want to go to, but that is usually followed by a day of being home by the RV where they can do what they want with nothing scheduled for the whole day.

We go to bed late. We sleep in. We cuddle in the morning, eat breakfast together, have pancakes on a Wednesday or make donuts from scratch. Everything is at our pace and it is a slower pace. It is freedom, it is independence.

It really is a beautiful thing and is a big part of what we do. Anyone you talk to with grown kids talks about how fast the time goes. We can see that happening. Our oldest just turned 10 years old. Wow! That went fast.

With our current lifestyle, we are all together as a family for most of the day. All 6 of us. Dad included. That is why we do this. It doesn't slow time down, yet in some ways it seems like it does. We aren't rushing from one thing to the next, but instead have hours of time in front of us each day.

We are Unschooling our kids. We have been really happy with the progress we have seen with the kids and are pleasantly surprised by how natural learning happens. Are our kids at the same level as kids in school? In the basics of reading, math and writing, probably not. But to be honest, we don't know what those levels even are or how or why they were created. Instead we gauge our kids as individuals and make sure they are progressing in learning. If they are, we are good with it. We have been happy to see each of them continue to progress at their own pace.

We are not anti-school. We think school is an amazing thing, and we know there are families and kids that need it, and we are happy that school is there as an option. Who knows, our kids may eventually end up in school. That isn't our plan, but our plans are also very open and flexible, so you never know.

We know some parents are excited when school starts again and they won't be with their kids 24/7 anymore. We also know parents that are sad about their kids going back to school. We would be lying if we said there weren't times we wish our kids went to school - it would mean more focused time for us to work. But the majority of the time, we feel so lucky to have our kids with us all day everyday, and to be able to explore this amazing world together as a family.

What better way to learn than to see, hear, touch, smell and taste all that this beautiful world has to offer. The basics will come, we aren't worried about it, in the meantime, the family bond and experiences are our priority and that works for us.

Our kids aren't in a grade, they don't take tests, they don't do worksheets (unless they want to). Yet they learn each and every day.

They throw out facts about things that we have no idea where they learned them from. Kids are sponges and they are learning even if they aren't in a school setting.

We live in an ever-changing world and we are hoping by taking this approach our kids are learning how to be adaptable, how to speak for themselves, how to only follow rules after questioning them and making sure they make sense, how to come up with their own ideas and ways to do things and how to think on their own.

Yes, it makes parenting more difficult. Our kids question us and challenge us at every turn. But we are hoping this makes our kids leaders, questioners and individual thinkers. Parents are always looking for the best situation for their kids and their family. Ours just ends up being a little different than the norm. That is why our world is such an amazing place. It is filled with people that have different beliefs and live life in their own ways. We can all learn so much from each other.

If your kids are in school, we hope they have an amazing year! If they aren't in school, we hope for the same thing! Above all, it is about enjoying our kids and making the most of our time with them.

Unschooling With Older Kids

Now our kids are 13, 11, 11 and 8. We have continued to Unschool them. They have still not had any formal education. We don't follow a curriculum and we don't normally do workbooks or worksheets. Once in a while we will pull out the workbooks/worksheets and we are always impressed by how much the kids do know. Here is our 100% honest review on it:

There are days we are really happy with how things are going and feel really good about what our kids have learned, are learning and what they do with their time.

There are other days we worry that we aren't giving them enough, and they need more formal education. But whenever we feel this, it just lasts a few hours or a day and then we are right back to feeling like this IS the right thing for us and our kids. We are super excited to see our kids grow and to see who they are evolving and changing into. We are also excited for the future and what this kind of upbringing and education will do for them. The doors it will open and the life they will live because of it.

Yes, there are successful adult Unschoolers out there who we can learn from and who demonstrate this method of "schooling" does work. But even without that, we can tell we are giving our kids a gift of control, open mindness and an ability to not need directions or to be told what to do. Given the pace that our world is moving at, we really see this as being a big benefit to them.

Reading, Writing, Math

I am sure you are wondering, but what about reading, writing and math? They don't just pick that up - right? Well, actually, they do! We have not done any formal reading training, yet all of our kids can read. How? Because they wanted to, so they figured out how to.

We did no formal handwriting with any of our kids. Yet they can all write. Some of them with neater handwriting than me! How? Because they wanted to know how so they learned on their own.

Math - They all know how to add, subtract, multiply and divide - because we did worksheets? No - because we talk about numbers and we talk about money and we answer their questions. Math is used so many times in normal life you are able to quickly learn how it works just by applying it in your daily life.

Science, Geography, History all happens on its own through conversations, movies, documentaries, National Parks, Junior Ranger Programs, museums. The list goes on and on!

In a nutshell, they are learning because they want to. Since they want to, they are better absorbing it and taking it in, rather than being forced to learn about things they don't really want to learn about.

Nonetheless, we still wonder sometimes if this is truly right for them. And then we may change our focus to put more effort into traditional school things. Like if we are staying in one place for a while, or haven't been doing a lot of exploring. We also understand that this isn't the right route for everyone, and you have to do what works for you and your family. Just make sure you are making the choice from a place of research and what feels right for your family and not because you are doing what you think you should be doing based on seeing what everyone else is doing. You made the choice to live an unconventional life, so why school in a conventional way?

Instead, put the focus on your kids, your relationship, healthy eating, snuggling, sleeping in late, being lazy and just enjoying this amazing journey you are on!

Unschooling Resources

Here are some of our favorite unschooling resources. Both of the women below have adult-aged kids who were Radically Uschooled.

- Sandra Dodd
- Pam Laricchia - https://livingjoyfully.ca/

I highly recommend subscribing to Pam's newsletter as well – you can do this via her site: https://livingjoyfully.ca/

She also does a great Podcast called Exploring Unschooling. I was on episode 92 where I talked about our journey with Unschooling.

Here are a few books that I recommend on Radical Unschooling:

- Life Through the Lens of Unschooling: A Living Joyfully

Companion - By Pam Laricchia

- Free to Live: Create a Thriving Unschooling Home - By Pam Laricchia
- Free to Learn: Five Ideas for a Joyful Unschooling Life - By Pam Laricchia
- The Unschooling Unmanual: Nurturing Children's Natural Love of Learning - By a variety of authors

I also belong to the Facebook group Unschooling Discussion (hosted by Sandra Dodd). I do NOT recommend joining this Facebook Group unless you are really serious about Radical Unschooling. And if you do decide to join don't worry about introducing yourself right away. Instead, read the rules of the group and do a LOT of reading, thinking, trying, and learning before you engage in the conversations.

It is Sandra Dodd's group and she is an amazing resource on Radical Unschooling. But she is not someone who is going to make you feel all warm and fuzzy about it. Instead, she drives people to really dig deep into what is going on in your family, with you, and with your kids. The reality is, it is usually more work for us parents to adjust to this style of learning than it is for the kids.

What I love about her group is it is real and raw and doesn't let people hide behind false ideas, but instead brings suggestions and ideas to the forefront and really makes us as parents think about how we want to raise and "school" our kids. I will be the first to say Radical Unschooling isn't for everyone. I will also say we have chosen to take and also leave some components of Radical Unschooling depending on what we learn as we figure out what works for our family. We also know it is a never-ending process and we are always evaluating, learning and adjusting what we do.

If you go out and look at any of these sites or join the Facebook Group, you will be able to find a lot of other resources as well. The neat thing about doing Unschooling and, even more so, with the Radical Unschooling aspect – is that both my husband and I get to grow and learn and dig deeper into who we are as people and as parents.

This route of homeschooling is more challenging for us than it is for our kids! They are doing what feels natural and right (since no one has told them otherwise!) But, we have to deschool and remember that learning is happening all day everyday all around us.

Enjoying Your Time On The Road

In the end our best advice - even if you aren't committed to the whole philosophy of Unschooling - is to enjoy your time on the road with your kids. Don't fill it with a tight schedule and hours of school work. Instead, fill it with lazy mornings, big breakfasts, reading on the couch, exploring outside, the beach for days on end, hiking a new trail every day. Fill it with things you couldn't do when you lived in a house!

Ideas For Fun Learning On The Road

Junior Ranger Programs - full disclosure - my kids are pretty much over them. If we are with friends who have never done it before, they may be interested in doing it. But for the most part they aren't. And that is OK. I would much rather be outside hiking at the National Park!

That being said, we do enjoy going into the Visitor Centers at National Parks so we can watch the movie about the park, check out the exhibits and learn about where we are at. But no need to fill out a workbook to feel like the kids learned something. Then again, if your kid is into the badge, go for it!

Museum Membership

The reciprocal museum membership has been amazing for us! It can get you into museums, aquariums, and zoos around the country for free or reduced pricing. With a family of 6 this is huge. When the kids were little, we did the membership with the children's museums on it and visited some pretty amazing Children's museums around the country!

Other Options For Homeschooling On The Road

I am well aware that Unschooling is not for everyone. For that reason, I reached out to Nicole Schroeder, the owner of Fulltime Families and mother to 3 children - currently 18, 14, and 12 - that she has homeschooled for the last 5+ years. They have also been traveling full time in their RV for the last 3+ years. Here is what Nicole had to say about schooling from the road:

"We started homeschooling our children when they were 7th grade, 4th grade, and 1st grade. To kick off our new adventure we took a two-week camping trip to South Dakota and learned so much about geography, history, and the excitement of learning. At the time we thought of it as a fun trip, but you'll see how it has come full circle. Throughout the years homeschool has taken many different forms for us and no two years have ever been the same.

Since my background is in education, our first years were mostly centered around curriculum. In the summer we would decide what we wanted to teach for the year and shipments of textbooks would start arriving. Math and Language Arts have stayed as more formal education for us over the years and we have been using Teaching Textbooks and IEW (Institute for Excellence in Writing). I always recommend Teaching Textbooks because it has instruction at the beginning of the lesson and then corrects each problem as the learner works through it. This is hands-off for the parent and allows for correction mid-lesson. Other subjects have been a mix of random curriculums, typically faith based.

Those first years we always started out strong but come Christmas time we were tired. Something had to give. Joining a co-op was a welcome change for our family. We were able to study some subjects with friends and I could rely on the expertise and passion of others for teaching subjects I was not as confident in or did not enjoy as much.

Those are some of our most treasured memories of our early homeschooling years.

One spring we took a month-long road trip to a few states we had not been to before and remembered how much we enjoyed learning in a less structured, more hands-on way. That trip led to the idea of taking our schooling on the road for a year to see more of the country. We wanted to see the earthworks of the battlefields, experience the special things that each state is known for, and allow actual people to teach us instead of just reading from textbooks. This started our journey of being a full-time traveling family. While it started out as an eight-month enrichment trip, it turned into a lifestyle that we absolutely love.

Math and Language Arts are still formal for us, but science, geography, history, P.E., and life skills are more natural. We have learned about Gettysburg by taking a tour and walking on the same ground as the soldiers. We have attended living history museums to hear about life back in the early 1900's. We have laid on our bellies on the dock in Alaska to identify marine life and understand the importance of each organism. We have toured factories to understand how things like Ford trucks, Buckeye candy, Burton snowboards, and many other items are made. We have explored countless state and national parks to see their uniqueness and listen to rangers share about the history and science within the park boundaries. We learned how to play pickleball with our Fulltime Families friends and when we attend events together, we do STEM challenges and art projects. We took a covered wagon ride on the Oregon Trail with a historian and slept in a teepee. We took the RV to Mexico to immerse ourselves in a different culture and then we flew to Europe to explore there and take our learning to a whole new level.

We have even volunteered to crew a hot air balloon so we could experience that community and that skill. If you seek out museums, aquariums, state and national parks, businesses, living history events, special happenings in the town you are in, and talk to people, your family can learn so much and have a richer learning experience because of it.

Roadschooling is what we do now, and it is what we will always do in some form.

As my children have gotten older, and one has now even graduated, we have supplemented in some ways. When our children are at the high school stage, they study general subjects that would be taken both in high school and in the first couple years of college. When they are proficient in a qualifying subject, they take a CLEP or DSST test and if they pass, they can submit that score to certain colleges to receive college credit for that class. It is basically like self-study and then testing out of the class. My oldest had around 20 credits by the time he was a junior and could take actual college classes.

Our home state of Minnesota has a program called PSEO, PostSecondary Education Options, and many other states participate and refer to it as Dual Enrollment. These programs allow high school juniors and seniors to apply to colleges and then take courses at the campus or online for free. Through the PSEO program my son was able to graduate high school with an Associate of Applied Science degree. Earning CLEP and DSST credits meant that he did not have to have a full load of courses every semester and we could still focus on our natural discoveries as well.

It is also important that we give credit to the casual conversations we have while driving in the car, swinging in the hammock, or walking around the campground. Conversations about health, compound interest, current events. We invite our children into our adult lives every day so we can teach them life skills. They shop with us, cook with us, do vehicle maintenance with us, and everything in between. We help them learn from our mistakes and allow them to navigate through theirs. Learning has become an integral part of our daily lives. Even when we aren't "schooling" we are still learning."

In Summary

There isn't just one way to homeschool while on the road, but instead a lot of different options and ways to do it. Plus a lot of it can ebb and flow as you are on the road and your kids are getting older.

I think the most important thing is let the kids be little as long as you can. They don't need to be doing any formal school when they are 5 or 6 (and I would say even older). Instead just talk to them during that time, read together, draw together, do fun things. Just enjoy your time with them.

I would even go as far as to say with older kids it can be the same way. I hate when I see parents on the road that are stressed about their kids having to do school every day. They end up missing out on amazing opportunities that are right outside their door because everyone is stressed and stuck at the table doing work.

There can be days this makes total sense and you just have to do that. But on days where an opportunity presents itself to go on an awesome "field trip" or even just to run out the door to play with new friends. Do it! Make that the focus. The things you and your kids will learn during these times are priceless.

Being at a campground has a lot of temptations. Your kids will want to run out the door in the morning to play. You will want to sit out on a weeknight with friends around the campfire. You will want to go back to the National Park for a 3rd day to keep exploring. My advice is - just do that! This is such a special part about this lifestyle. Don't miss out on it because you are stuck in your old life routines. This is your new life. These are your choices now. It is OK to go off the schedule and miss a day or week of school.

Don't stress about it. Instead, find the magic and the joy in all of these moments. They really are just as important as sitting at a table doing worksheets. Maybe more important. Embrace this new form of learning that is in front of you every day in this lifestyle. No, it can't be quantified or graded, but I guarantee there is a lot of learning and magic happening in these moments!

This leads into the next chapter that is all about changing your perspective. Not just on school but on life and how you want to approach things in this new lifestyle.

Chapter 12

Changing Your Perspective

For me and my hopes with this book, this is one of the most important sections. It is all about your mindset for your life on the road with your kids.

What are you envisioning? Taking your life from home on the road with you? Or making this whole transition about an actual life change in more ways than just that your house is on wheels.

We have seen time and time again that families bring their old life and routines with them on the road. I get it. It is comfortable; it has been working (or maybe not), but it is what you are used to.

Let me challenge you with this. What would you like to see differently in your life on the road? Think outside of the box. If you could imagine your "perfect" life - in quotes for a reason since perfect does not and should not exist - what would it look like?

Is it having coffee with your husband every morning sitting outside? Is it snuggling on the couch with your kids and watching movies together or reading a book? Is it not ever having to open a workbook and struggle with math with your kids again? Really think about it. What does your ideal day look like?

With this lifestyle change, you can make that ideal day happen! The first step comes with defining what you want that day to look like and then accepting that it is totally okay to have your life and days look like that even if no one else you know lives like that.

You are choosing to live this unconventional lifestyle of traveling and living full-time in an RV, so why not choose to live a life that is unconventional too?

I feel this is the most freeing aspect of this life of full-time RV travel with your family. The ability to make your day exactly how you want it to be. No judgment from the neighbors - since your neighbors are always changing. No judgment from teachers or coaches - since your kids most likely won't have any while traveling. The only judgment you will have is from yourself.

I understand that can be the hardest judgment to get past, but I challenge you to do it. Look deep inside and figure out what you want, and make it happen.

This means your kids may sleep in every day until 9 or 10 am and wake up and snuggle on the couch with you for an hour, and your official day doesn't start until 11 or 12. Guess what? That is 100% OK!

This means your kids may not do any math worksheets the whole time you are on the road. Yes, you read that right - NO math worksheets for the whole time you are on the road. Guess what? That is 100% OK! Instead, spend your time talking to your kids about math. Work it into your regular conversations when you go to the grocery store or when making dinner. The opportunities to talk about math and relate it to your day come up over and over again.

This means your kids may not have the same school skills as friends back home going to regular school - WHO CARES?! Your kids are gaining so many amazing skills by being with you all day, traveling and living a life outside of the school structure.

This means you may have breakfast at 11 am and skip lunch for an early dinner. Again, 100% OK! This is your life, so live it how you want to. Not how society, your extended family or social media is "telling" you to.

This means your kids may go on their electronics for 3, 4, 5 hours a day. Again, 100% OK! It is a nice way for Mom and Dad to have a break and spend time together, which is just as important, if not more, than many things in your family's life.

Make the things that matter really truly matter and give them a priority and let everything else go.

This life can be so freeing and life-changing, if you let it be. But you have to be willing to be open to change and allow yourself to feel a bit uncomfortable for a while.

Old habits and feelings that what you are doing aren't "right" will continue to sneak in. But remember, this is YOUR life now. You chose to leave the rat race and hit the road with your family. Why stop now! Make the change complete by changing your day-to-day life and how things work within your family.

Above all, ENJOY this journey you are on. Don't stress about school, bedtimes, showers, being clean 100% of the time. RELAX and enjoy being with your family; the adventures that you are going on; and this amazing lifestyle change you have embarked on! The time goes fast - faster than you think. Please, don't waste it fighting with the kids or each other about things that don't really matter.

Go back to the basics and soak in the glorious feeling of letting go of so many of these responsibilities and just enjoying your life and your family.

Of course, you still have to cook, clean, grocery shop, etc. But it is amazing how little time that really takes in your day and how much free time you have together as a family to be engaged, explore, or try a new project or hobby, if you open up your time and space to it.

It is so hard for me to see so many families trying to bring their life from home on the road. By doing that, you have only accomplished one step in this amazing journey.

So don't stop there! Keep changing- moving away from your preconceived notions of what life with kids is supposed to look like and start living the life you want in all aspects of your day - not just what your home looks like.

In the next chapter I'll talk about something that is so important to making this lifestyle enjoyable for everyone in your family.

Chapter 13

Finding Community

Finding Community while on the road is one of the most enjoyable things you can do. Don't discount this part of the experience. Sure, in the beginning, it can be fun to go off with your family to explore and travel, but becoming part of a community is like icing on the cake!

Community isn't just about friendships for the kids. It's also about friendships for the adults. It is interesting how when we lived in a house, it was so much harder to hang out with other adults. All the planning, driving to someone else's house, etc., was overwhelming. And after a week of working, it felt like a lot of work to make that happen on the weekend. In full-time RV life, it's so much easier!

You can just walk out your RV and join friends next door or down the road. No driving needed! This also means that the kids can play from sun up to sun down rather than just a couple of hours after school before it gets dark or they have to do homework. Literally, all day. And the nice thing is you are right there - so you can chat with the other parents, sit outside and work or read, or engage with the kids play, all right from your very own "front yard" at the RV campground.

Because we have been on the road since our kids were 6, 4, 4, and 2, they think this is normal life, and spending 10 hours playing with your friends is what everyone does. They are living an old-school neighborhood childhood. And the neighborhoods change with each campground, further enriching the experience.So how do you go about finding this community? You look for it; you put yourself out there; you make it happen.

If you want to go on the road with your family and never interact with another family or other people, you can 100% do this! Especially if you prefer boondocking or going to places off the beaten path. It is totally possible not to see or talk to other people for weeks at a time.

If this doesn't appeal to you and your family and you would rather be surrounded by other families and people all the time, you can also do this! It is all about being intentional with where you go and putting yourself out there a bit to meet people.

In our case, we have gone both ways to some extent. BUT our situation is a bit different. My sister and her family are on the road full time, and they have 2 kids who are not just cousins, but best friends, with our kids. Plus, my parents are on the road full time. So there have been times that our family group has just gone off and done our own thing together for months at a time.

So no, it isn't being without anyone. But we can happily take our family group and get away from it all!

In other situations, we have opted to go out and meet new people so our kids can make new friends and we can find new friendships as well.

About a year and a half ago, we decided that we wanted to make meeting other families on the road a priority. At this point, we had been on the road for over 5 years, so it became less about going to all the places we wanted to visit and more about going where people were that we wanted to hang out with. Also, with our kids at the ages they were at at the time: 12, 10, 10, and 8, it made sense to do this for them.

Below are some of the ways that we went about finding these friendships.

Fulltime Families

Fulltime Families is a group we have belonged to since we started full-timing almost 7 years ago. It is a community for any families on the road (or thinking about getting on the road) that are full-time RVing. As mentioned before, they have a free Facebook group you can join. If you buy a membership to Fulltime Families, you get added to the paid Facebook group and all community subgroups.

Belonging to Fulltime Families makes it so easy to meet other people. They have subgroups on Facebook that are specific to locations. For example, they have a Fulltime Families Florida group. So anyone that is in Florida can join that group. The groups are active, and people are always posting about where they are or where they are headed. And most people on there are looking to connect, too!

Like I had mentioned above, you have to put yourself out there a bit. So, if someone posts about being somewhere, you have to chime in and say: Hey! We are here. Want to meet up for a fire? Or post yourself if you are looking for other people to connect with.

We have come and gone from the Fulltime Families group throughout the years we have been on the road. But any time we know we are looking to meet new people and new friends, we know the Fulltime Family community is the place to go and will make that easy.

Rallies

Fulltime Families also host multiple rallies, hangouts and meetups throughout the year. This is like 40 instant friends! These rallies are crazy, amazing and so much fun! Imagine a block party with 30+ families that goes on for a week or more. Kids running around from sunup to sundown, events going on, campfires for the adults every night. SO MUCH FUN!!

This is another straightforward way to meet new people on the road. We have actually heard from multiple families that a Fulltime Family rally saved their full-time journey. They were out on the road feeling so lonely and lost. Then they went to a rally, and everything changed. They met friends, made ongoing relationships, and their full-time journey took a turn for the better.

We always recommend to anyone who is just going on the road that they find a rally ASAP. Just be prepared. They are overwhelming at first since there are so many people there - but this is also what makes them awesome. We would recommend not working, doing school or planning anything else for the rally week.

Fulltime Families also runs smaller size events called Meetups or Hang Outs. With these, there are fewer organized activities and usually fewer families. This can be a great option if there isn't a rally nearby or coming up soon.

Thousand Trails

As I touched on in Chapter 8 - Thousand Trails, is a campground membership plan. Once you have the membership, you can stay for "free" at their campgrounds around the US. This is good for budgeting, but also amazing for meeting other families!

Many families traveling full-time in an RV with kids and staying at campgrounds have a Thousand Trails membership. This means that when you go to a Thousand Trails campground, there are usually kids all over the place!

Thousand Trails can sometimes be a mini-rally that no one planned!

Tip: Go to Thousand Trails Orlando in January, and you will be camping with 40+ families for the next 2 weeks!

Thousand Trails campgrounds are an easy way to find other full-time RVing families on the road.

We bought our Thousand Trails membership after being on the road for about 7 months. We bought a used Elite membership - by buying used, we paid about 50% less than buying new. It has worked out great for us. If interested, you can try out Thousand Trail campgrounds without being a member.

Social Media

This was not as much of an option when we first started since there weren't as many people on the road. But now that so many more families are getting on the road, it is a great way to meet other like-minded families.

If you go onto Instagram and search by a hashtag like #fulltimervfamily and start looking through the posts, you can find accounts you enjoy and families you think would be a good fit with your family. This can be based on beliefs, kid's ages, jobs, etc.

To start building a friendship, comment on posts or stories and engage with their content. Send a direct message to introduce yourself and get the conversation going. Who knows, you may even be traveling to the same place soon!

For me, personally, this hasn't always worked. I much prefer meeting people at rallies or campgrounds in person. But I know for many families, Social Media has been where they have found friends and built amazing relationships.

Caravanning

We love caravanning with other families. The first winter we were on the road, we met 2 other families in Florida - one at a rally and one at Thousand Trails Orlando. We started our own caravan and ended up traveling together to a variety of places in Florida for the next 3 months.

We have done this with my sister's family and my parents through

Baja, Mexico, and multiple other places. We traveled with our friends from Australia up the west coast. Now with our friends Zula Life, we have been all over the US, and to their home country of Israel.

The funny thing with Zula Life; we parked next to each other at a rally in New Mexico. We talked a few times during the rally, but didn't see each other for another year. Then we met up again and parked next to each other at a rally in Texas. Since that rally in Texas, we have spent more of the year together than apart!

There is something so unique and fun about caravanning with people. Who else in their adult life spends hours with their friends every day! The kids become more like family than friends, and play from sunup to sundown. And the parents help each other out with rig fixes, supervising kids, and work. We share multiple meals a week and end almost every day with a drink or tea around the fire.

It is one of our favorite parts of this full-time RVing journey, and one of the reasons we can't imagine not living this way.

So, there you have a few ways that you can find community on the road. But let me repeat, this normally doesn't just happen. You do have to put in the effort. You do have to put yourself out there. You may have to change plans to go where the community you are looking for is. But it is worth it. If having a community is important to you, then put the effort in and make it happen.

Remember, most people out there are looking for community, too, so don't worry about feeling stupid or weird walking over to introduce yourself to someone or reaching out via social media. They will most likely be happy you reached out! Once you have made that initial connection, put time and effort in. Send a text inviting them over for a campfire. Give them a call to see if they want to go for a walk. Work on the friendship and watch it grow into an amazing relationship for you and your family!

Alright, so community is great and all, but what about alone time and time with your partner/spouse. And what about having Sex in the RV - can that even work?! More on that in the next chapter!

Chapter 14

Sex Time, Alone Time and Couple Time

This question comes up all the time! Even if it isn't asked, you know people are wondering . . . how the heck do you have sex in an RV with all thoses kids in there with you?!

We always smile (secretly laughing) and tell them the truth - when you are with your significant other 24/7 you want it a lot more! At least that is the case for us. So you figure out how to make it work.

In a lot of RVs there is a separate bedroom. Just like in a house. So you would carry on just like you do in a house. Not much changes.

Most RV bedrooms do not have a lock on the door - not sure why?? But it is one of the things we put on right away when we move into a new rig.

When the kids were smaller we were in some small rigs so it was a bit different. But being smaller, they were also less aware of what was going on. With older kids we know we need/want a door barrier that can be locked.

When we had a smaller rig we would just have a curtain up separating our bed from where they were sleeping. Yes, it can be weird at first, but you get used to it. Think back when everyone lived in 1 room houses . . . the kids were just used to it. It was natural.

Still, we always made sure there was some sort of barrier up AND that the kids were totally asleep. As they got older, that got harder which meant we wanted a rig with a separate bedroom for us with locks on the door.

There are also tricks like running your washer and dryer so that the rig is shaking and there is additional noise. We have also always used white noise so it is harder to hear everything. Recently we got MORryde stabilizers added to our 5th wheel which helps, too!

So it is 100% possible and your sex life does not have to suffer AT ALL. If anything, it may get better. I know ours did once we got on the road!

Besides sex, there is also just alone time. This is definitely hard to come by in your RV. The space is just that much smaller. You don't have a ton of extra space and it is super easy for the kids or your partner to find you.

Like with anything, if you are intentional about it you can make it happen. It may just be a walk around the campground by yourself. Or driving to the beach or a hiking trail. Again, if it is something that you want and is important to you, don't ignore it. Make it happen.

It is also a good conversation to have with your partner to make sure you are both getting the time and space you need. Don't ignore this. Address it and address it soon so it can be part of your daily life.

Same goes for couple's time. When you are away from your family and friends it can be hard to find a babysitter. Here are a few options we have tried.

- Put the kids to bed and set up a date night out on your picnic table or watch a movie back in your room. Sure, this isn't anything extravagant, but is still worth including in your day. Don't lose sight of your relationship with your partner. It is important for both of you and for your family.
- As you meet friends on the road and start to build your

community, you can tap into that and take turns watching each other's kids a few hours a week.

- Hire another traveling family's teenager to watch the kids.

My parents and sister also travel full-time so that has been helpful for us - but I know that isn't normal.

All of this doesn't need to be much different from back home, but you just have to put in a bit more effort to figure out how to make it happen. But it is possible and important and should be a priority.

We also try to have our own little date nights when the kids are on their electronics or watching a movie. You just have to find those times and space when you can do it.

For this subject I wanted to bring in an expert because this should be an important point of discussion before you begin this lifestyle!

Let me introduce Ashley. We met Ashley years ago in Austin, Texas, when her husband rode his bike by our campsite and stopped to ask if we were full time RVers. We sat around the fire that night and would reconnect multiple times over the years!

I have listened to her podcasts, and Craig and I have taken her personality tests to help with our marriage. One thing that impressed me was when Ashley would talk about how she and her husband Nathan spent a year where they had sex every day. Say what?! Craig was all ears when I mentioned that!

She talked about how they always make sure to make their relationship a priority and spend time every night together talking, hanging out, touching. It was inspiring and opened my eyes to the importance of making our physical relationship as much a priority as anything else in our life and relationship.

Needless to say, when this chapter came up - since I know a lot of people are wondering how this all works in a tiny RV - I knew I needed to reach out to Ashley to see if she was interested in contributing to this chapter. She said yes right away and I am excited to share what she had to say!

Ashley takes families from surviving to thriving by helping them uncover how "the uniqueness in each of us strengthens all of us." She guides parents through identifying their strengths - and also their triggers so that they can learn to live with intention and not simply react to the chaos of an ever-growing family. Through her podcast, blogging, coaching (both business and personal) and personality "snapshots", she provides tools and action steps to aid families in creating the life they love to come home to. You can check out her site here: https://www.mamasaysnamaste.com/

Here is what Ashley has to say on sex and relationships while full-time RVing:

"Warning. This will be oversharing. This may be your first introduction to who I am, so let me preface this by saying that I'm a pretty open book! As a relationships coach, I work with families and professionals to move from basic communication to true connection in their home...and beyond. I work with families to create the life story they all thrive in. And that definitely takes into account every family member. We don't have a child-centered home, and we don't have a parent-only one.

In our family-centered home, right now that includes my husband of 16 years, our three daughters, ages 13, 11 and 8, our dog, two kittens, and four - yes, four - snakes. And where do we live the majority of the time, you ask? "Home" is our 35-foot Jayco Eagle 5th wheel, traveling wherever we please in the US. Honestly, home is wherever we are, so this house on wheels is our homiest of homes! We've been on the road since 2016, and in the first two years hit all lower 48 states.

So let's cut to the chase - the biggie I get asked isn't about where to go on your RV travels - my friend Bryanna has plenty of great ideas on that one! As I focus so often on marriage and family, the question is how in the world do you have space for yourself - and intimate space for you and your partner - when you are on the road?

Well, here is my segue into oversharing. While I could share so much about the way we unschool on the road as the "FieldTripGypsies", or how to pace yourself to allow for downtime...I bet your mind is already on the logistics of how intimacy works with a family zoo in less than 240 square feet.

I tell you what you do. You get creative! When our children were little, early bedtimes were our best friend. Also, movies - especially loud ones - can keep their attention for a little private 1-1 time.

As they've grown, well, we're an open book. It's no question that we make love a lot. And yet...I am shocked at how little my 13-year-old actually thinks we're having sex! For being in such small quarters, with a very observant little eavesdropper, it's really come to my attention that what happens behind closed doors is often times really unknown.

While I may be freaking out about getting caught, my kids are oblivious. They are focused on their work, playing, sleeping, or otherwise doing their own thing. The older they've gotten, the more time I have available without them needing me.

So while in an RV, same as a "sticks & bricks" house, you can explore many avenues here! Look beyond just the bedroom at night. Maybe early mornings are when the rig is in the deepest sleep, or, when the kids are outside playing, you have a perfect "afternoon meeting" that needs to happen inside the rig. Maybe you go back to the 70s and run out with just your partner to do some necking in the car.

In regard to the shaking that may occur, well, first off, creativity can also be exploring new positions you hadn't tried before! And, the camper shakes for many, many reasons. Maybe there is dancing going on, or a washing machine...or super windy outside.

Sometimes switching it up to getting intimate when our children are bouncing around, physically active and distracted. Kids lost in their own adventures oftentimes aren't paying attention to ours.

And what about a lock, you say? Lock or no lock, my kids are taught respect when entering someone's area, and knocking is enforced - even when we had a curtain, they would tap at the wall! So we try to all respect knocking - and waiting - before entering. That being said, explain that to a 2-year-old. Sometimes installing a simple lock can help to give you enough time to notice what's going on, and definitely ease your fears about any accidental walk-ins!

Sometimes, we create a much bigger hub-bub around something that is completely natural. Our children, these animal-loving kids who are out in nature all the time, they are seeing intimacy in nature every day. It is a natural and beautiful thing, and it can translate to what goes on in our own homes. Like Bryanna said in the intro, being together 24/7 with your partner can definitely open the door to becoming more intimate - on top of the closeness that can happen from being together all the time - you literally have more time to make it happen!

Physical touch, when done in pure openness and love, can bridge a connection even if you are at an impasse in the relationship. Sometimes, words are too much. Sometimes, you simply need to touch. We often say that it's hard to be emotionally distant when you physically connect on a daily basis. So clearly, making room for all kinds of touch - including that wonderful sexual intimacy - is important.

You have to be intentional. You have to get out of your comfort zone and recognize why you feel it's a priority in your relationship...and then prioritize it.

There are always excuses, always circumstances that come up, always, always, something that is not perfect. If you only wait for the perfect tropical sunset, all children to be sweetly sleeping in their beds, and the RV in immaculate condition, your sexy night may never happen.

So our children see us hug and kiss and massage each other. They overhear conversations we have that are between us, and even hear when we disagree. We are living life with them, and they are learning how to "adult" as they see us live out our own lives. And, just like I'm not calling up my mother to see how many times she made love to my father last week, they aren't really prying into exactly what all we're doing behind closed doors.

When the door is so often open for them, and they are getting support and open conversation with us all the time, it makes it way easier to have a clear boundary when the door is shut. Now, reach out and touch your partner!"

So there you have it! Sex is possible in an RV, and living in an RV with your spouse can lead to even more intimacy and connection than living in a sticks and bricks house with a huge bedroom!

Next I talk about how we manage (or don't) running 2 businesses while raising 4 kids and traveling full-time. It isn't always pretty!

Chapter 15

How We Manage (or Don't) Working From The Road With Kids

Working with kids around 24/7 has its challenges, but is doable. You just need to be willing to be a bit flexible.

Right out of the gate, I will be totally honest. We don't really know how to do this! It is a constant conversation and ebb and flow in our life. We are always working on it. When the kids were 9, 7, 7, and 5 Virtual Powerhouse was doing well and growing, and the blog was starting to take off.

We had switched the focus to where I was responsible for bringing in most of the income - Craig still had a few side projects he would do, but most of the income was coming from me through Virtual Powerhouse and Crazy Family Adventure.

Why did we decide to switch focus? Well, seriously, we wanted to stay married and still like each other!

Have you ever tried starting a business with your spouse?? We found it wasn't easy! Craig and I were high school sweethearts. We literally grew up together. We were dating each other before we could drive.

Our relationship has always been intense and intertwined, where we do pretty much everything together, and enjoy spending downtime together. We don't spend much time apart. And we like it that way.

Adding building a business together into the mix pushed us and stretched us. We have very different personalities. I am a Type A person who wants control and goes at 100 miles a minute, and I have a hard time sitting still or settling. Craig is much more laid back and enjoys diving deep into a topic and understanding it before moving ahead.

Not the perfect combination when you are trying to start multiple businesses . . . I had expectations based on how I would do it. And he had expectations based on how he would do it. And guess what? They didn't match.

This was HARD. There were times we'd fight, and just plain didn't like each other. It was a struggle to find common ground where we both felt like our needs were being met. And where we felt like we were bringing the best out of each other at a professional and personal level.

Starting a business with your spouse and sitting across the table from each other, working and busting our butts, can be so rewarding. Having this freedom to do what we wanted, be what we wanted, go where we wanted was fantastic. But man, it was challenging, frustrating, and confusing.

At that time we went through one of the most challenging points in our marriage. We looked at each other and wondered if we were going to be able to make this work, did it make sense, and what the heck were we doing to each other?!

Luckily for us, and because of our deep love for each other, we knew we wanted to make it work. We knew there was no other option. Our relationship was more important than any business, money or accomplishments.

Does that mean all of a sudden, things became perfect? No, of course not. But it meant we worked through it, said our apologies, talked about what we both needed and talked about a plan on how to make that work. Then we had to implement it.

Craig and I are and have always been very open with each other and share pretty much everything. Yes, he is a typical guy who doesn't like to communicate. And yes, I can be a nagging wife who won't take a vague answer. But I think that over-communication is what continues to help us through these situations.

We won't let things dwell; we don't want to feel disconnected; we want to know what the other person is thinking. So we keep working at it. And each time we go through this, we come out the other end knowing each other better, our relationship is stronger, and we are one step closer to realizing our dreams together as a couple.

Before considering starting a business with your spouse, we recommend the following:

- Know that you will disagree a lot, but don't let that stop you from communicating.
- If someone isn't happy about how things are going, say something - but in a pleasant, open, non-defensive manner.
- Talk through a plan each week, so each person knows where the other person is at for that week.
- Realize if something goes wrong on either end, it is always better to support each other vs. adding more pressure to the person that may have messed up.
- When push comes to shove, LOVE each other. It doesn't mean you always have to like each other, but you should never forget that you love each other and that is what matters. Then work as hard as possible to get back to liking each other.
- Always kiss each other good night, even if you disagree.

Working with your significant other can be a rewarding and fantastic process. And it can deepen your bond, but it will be a bumpy ride - so do what you can to enjoy it!

However, we found there just wasn't much joy for either of us working together and trying to "split" the responsibilities.

Instead, we chose to have me take on the role of the primary breadwinner. We did this for a couple of reasons.

One - I love being an entrepreneur. I love putting myself out there, coming up with new ideas, pitching my services or brand. The challenge is exhilarating, and I thrive in it. Craig - not so much! He was a fantastic employee/manager at all of his jobs, and everyone loved him. But when it comes to being an entrepreneur, it just isn't his gig.

Two - Virtual Powerhouse brings in a consistent income. My clients pay a monthly fee. This means we have a pretty good idea of how much money we are making each month. This is much easier to manage than Craig doing Web Design, where the work is all project-based.

To save our marriage and relationship, we talked and decided we would give this a go. Craig would take on more of the homeschooling, being with the kids during the day, and the cooking and cleaning. I would focus on building the businesses. All with the mindset that I still just wanted to work 20 hours a week. Even if that meant our businesses wouldn't grow as quickly as they could. Our time has always been more important than money.

Craig would also still be the in-house IT guy to help with backend things on our websites. And he would still write blog posts or help with YouTube videos. Plus, he'd be a part of the Podcasts and overall business strategy.

OK, so that is the long answer of how we got to this point. This lifestyle and entrepreneur world is a fun, exciting, and scary roller coaster ride!!

Alright, let's go back a few years - with updates added to compare it to where we are now:

I was internally having this struggle about being the Mom I wanted to be and enjoying and loving being an entrepreneur. When I worked a 9 to 5 job, before kids, I worked hard at it and did well, but I was done when the day was done. I didn't bring work home.

Being a digital nomad/entrepreneur was so different since the office was home, and home was the office. It was a lot harder for me to stop working at the end of the day when there wasn't an end to the day per se. It had to be a conscious decision for me to stop. And man, that was harder than I thought!

I have had constant guilt around enjoying growing my business, being an entrepreneur, seeing success with the blog, and wanting to continue to pursue that. Launching the course and wanting to advertise that more, getting our YouTube channel going, starting a podcast, and the list went on and on. And I enjoyed doing all of this.

BUT, I also really wanted to be the best Mom I could be, I wanted to unschool our kids, I wanted to just hang out with them, I wanted to hang out with Craig, I wanted to be lazy (sometimes - I do have a hard time sitting still!)

The thing for me was I had a hard time doing something halfway. If my mind was focused on my business, I tended to think about it ALL the time. And I found more and more, that was the direction my head was going.

Maybe it was because I had been a full-time Mom (exclusively breastfeeding all four until they were over three years old, co-sleeping, no daycare, no school, etc.) for almost ten years. Don't get me wrong, I wouldn't change a thing about the way we did things, but I was starting to see a side of me that wanted to be more ME and not just the Mom.

Figuring out how I could do that and still parent the way we wanted to with four kids had been a challenge and continues to be a challenge.

When the kids were at a campground with friends or family and were occupied, I tried to jump right on my computer and take advantage of that time. The problem was that I then had a hard time stopping when they came to ask me for something. That was that whole "not doing things halfway" thing. If I started, I wanted to finish.

However, I also wanted to be there for the kids when they wanted me. It was hard not to resent them for the interruptions. But I chose to focus on NOT resenting them and responding to their needs. But man, was it hard!!

I had multiple entrepreneur moms tell me that I should never use the word balance. Because balance is an elusive thing that just does not exist. I have to say, when I heard this, I felt a sense of relief.

I had been trying so hard to find that magical balance. This searching was taking away from every aspect of my life. Letting that go allowed me to look into each day and figure out what needed to change to make it work the way I wanted it to.

The whole reason we began this lifestyle was to be closer as a family and to spend time deepening our family bond. At the time, we weren't planning on starting a business and didn't truly understand everything that went into traveling full-time (there is a whole lot of work and planning - all the time!!).

Like I mentioned above, this is the ebb and flow. We did start a business, and for it to be successful, we have had to put time and focus into it. We are not on vacation - we need money to live and to continue this lifestyle.

In the beginning, I worked a lot and found that most of that time was spent at night when everyone else was asleep. That worked well for a while, but 4 hours of sleep a night is not maintainable or healthy. Plus, I like to hang out with Craig at night when the kids are sleeping and watch TV or a movie.

Plus, we had committed to unschool our kids, and it was a big commitment and not something we took lightly, so we wanted to be sure we were putting the time and focus into that.

I know every parent out there feels the pressure of so many balls to juggle, and we all strive for that magical balance. Instead, I started focusing on making sure I was doing what I wanted to do every day while still making the kids a priority.

Here is how I strove to do that. Let me preface this by saying I DID NOT always do an excellent job with this. Especially #2. If I was focused and doing something, I had a hard time switching my focus to the kids - but I worked on it.

I had ONE day a week that was all about work for me. That was the day I told the kids, "Mommy is working; go ask Daddy". Yes, I said that over and over again, but eventually, they figured it out. Or, if it made sense, I would go to Starbucks to work.

Having this one day allowed me to schedule calls and focus instead of just working in bits and pieces across multiple days.

On days I got a full day of work, we didn't plan outings, travel, etc., and I could get the bulk of my work done for my clients in that one day.

**UPDATE - it has been a few years since I wrote this post, and both of our businesses have since grown. For that reason, I don't do just one day a week anymore but, instead, find that working 2-5 hours a day works better to manage my workload and be there to help the kids with learning. I also now have an Operations Manager and Team Leader for Virtual Powerhouse, which is a huge help and takes a lot of the workload off of me. I also have a virtual assistant and occasional writers for Crazy Family Adventure. Ebb and flow is the name of the game!!

On the other days of the week, I tried to choose my kids over everything else. If they wanted to do something, I made that a priority. If they wanted to snuggle, read a book, or show me something, I tried to stop what I was doing to be with them.

I still felt I needed work in this area, but being aware of it helped me see the times I would say - wait, in a little bit, or not right now. And I tried to change that.

I also found that if we could get out of the RV as a family and go somewhere, my focus was so much more on them and not on work or things that needed to be done around the RV.

Our traveling suffered as we figured this all out. We would go to locations and not do all the cool things we could or wanted to do because we just hadn't planned enough in advance. Or didn't even know what there was to do in the area.

From a priority standpoint, this took the back burner for a little while, and we tried to figure out how to make it work better. We talked about planning a few road trips where we would do all the bookings and activity planning ahead of time - like months ahead of time. Then we wouldn't miss the things we wanted to do and didn't have to be worried about daily planning. On the other hand, we liked that our life was flexible, and things could quickly change day in and day out. But I thought trying the road trip planning would let us see how that worked for our family going forward.

We were flexible. This was so key to making this life a reality. This meant there could be days I had to work after the kids go to bed. Or times I was working as we were driving in the car to the grocery store.

It was changing plans or adjusting things so we could meet deadlines. It was OK because every situation wasn't set up to be ideal, yet if we wanted it bad enough, we would make it work.

When I looked into the future, I thought we should be focusing on streamlining the things we were doing. I tended to jump from idea to idea without getting a good process and plan in place. If we could focus on the process and the plan, we would accomplish so much more in less time and without the struggles!

We had learned how to simplify our life by having fewer things. We were deepening our family bond by spending a lot of time together and pushing to make this our top priority. We would also keep a pulse on our business and the blog to ensure we didn't take on more than what we

WANTED to do.

The best advice I can give (for you and me to read every day!) is to not lose sight of what you WANT to do in your day. Don't lose sight of your priorities, and make sure to catch yourself from going down a route that will back you into a corner (like having to work more to make more money because we are spending too much!).

Our WANTS and our WHY (to deepen our family bond) for traveling full-time has helped us multiple times to realign the direction we are going. We live our lives the way we WANT to, not the way someone else or society tells us. But man, that pull is always there!

Up next is a chapter about what happens when things go wrong. Like when your rig breaks down on the highway with cars and semi's whipping past you!

Chapter 16
When Things Go Wrong

It will happen . . . but you figure it out. Here is what happened when we broke down on the highway.

When we broke down a few years ago, we were in Huntsville, AL. We said we were so lucky that we had a car with us, that we were close to places we could take the rig in, and that it happened on a side road by a parking lot.

Then it happened again . . . this time on I80, in the middle of nowhere, in Iowa on the highway with no car. Yup - all the things we said helped with the last time we didn't have this time. That's full-time RV living for you!

Here's the story:

After leaving an excellent $15 a night campground called Arrowcreek outside Omaha, Nebraska, we were cruising down the highway. Excited to get to Illinois to an RV park where we could hook up for the night, blast some AC (it was like 100 degrees outside and no AC in the RV while we are driving), do some laundry, take showers, and fill up our water before heading to meet Craig's family for a boondocking camping weekend.

Then the noise. You know when you hear a noise, and you just hope it goes away. It didn't go away. Craig and I looked at each other and decided he needed to pull over. I finished typing out a message as he went to check. I thought it wasn't a big deal. . .

I grabbed my shoes and jumped out to see what's up, and there is fluid all over the ground under the RV. Well, that can't be good! The semis and cars are flying by us, and the whole RV is shaking. We knew we couldn't drive it - I did ask Craig just in case, since I could see a gas station up ahead, but he gave a firm NO, which was the right choice!

We both went back to the RV and started packing up a backpack, water, ipads, and a few snacks. We didn't know what was going to happen next, but we just wanted to get the kids off of the side of the highway.

To do that, we had to walk through waist-high tall grass with who knows what crawling around in it to a barbed-wire fence. Craig lifted the kids and Indy (our dog) over. Both Craig and I were able to put a hand on the railing and climb over. Then we walked up to a dirt road.

The dirt road went nowhere. I could see the truck stop/gas station up ahead, but we couldn't see how to get to it. I Googled it on my phone, and it was a 2 1/2 mile or hour-long walk. Did I mention it was 100 degrees outside.

Since getting back from Canada, Craig's phone had not been working well, so he had no service. That meant we had one phone with 50% battery power left. We Googled Dodge Dealers and started to call to see which ones would service our RV (it has a Dodge Sprinter Chassis).

We got hold of what we thought was the closest one, and they said they could get us in on Monday. It was Wednesday. Like seriously. . . we are stranded on the side of the road here. We called another place, and after being on hold for about 20 minutes, we finally found out that they could get us in the next morning. The only problem was, it was 1 hour away from where we were. . .

Craig called Roadside Assistance and found out we have a 45-mile tow range. Well, this place was 65 miles away. So we would have to pay the $100 difference. Whatever, let's just go. The problem was the tow truck driver did not have a place for all 6 of us and a dog . . . One problem at a time. Let's just get the tow truck here and figure that out.

When the guy got there, he recommended a closer Dodge place about 18 miles away (it didn't

show up on Google search since Dodge wasn't in the name). We called, and they said sure they could get us in tomorrow morning. The tow truck driver also offered to have me and the kids ride in the RV while it was being towed. At this point, that sounded just fine. Was it the safest? No - but sitting out in the 100-degree heat wasn't either. Plus, the kids would be buckled in their seats. The ride wasn't that bad at all.

Luckily, the place was on a back road, so we didn't have to go on the highway like that. We got to the place he recommended and didn't have to pay the additional $100! The service manager and their whole team were so nice and helpful when we got there. They brought us and our dog water and offered to run an extension cord out to the RV, so we had some power.

They even had a minivan that they would loan us! We had pretty much decided we would just stay in the RV overnight rather than pay for a hotel (note: check your roadside assistance and see how much it costs to get a plan that includes a rental car and hotel stay).

As we rounded the corner to go back to the RV, we saw some guys working on it. We hurried over there to see what they were doing - maybe it was an easy fix!

The guys were pulling the belt off that had ripped apart and found that it had hit a transmission line - which was why there was fluid all over the ground. The service manager had one of their guys call the owner of the parts store down the street (it had just closed), so they could get the parts they needed to fix it.

We hung out there just hoping that it would be an easy fix. By this time, it was 5 pm - when everyone should have headed home. But instead, these guys stayed and continued to work on it. The whole time they were working on it, we could see a storm moving in, and they had mentioned how there had been a tornado the night before . . . yes, the story gets better and better.

Two hours later, they had the new belt on, the line patched up, new transmission fluid in, and everything seemed to be running well. The service manager went to take it for a test drive, and the minute he drove off the lot, a massive gust of wind came from the storm, and we all ran into the building.

We kept thinking this guy is driving our RV out there in this weather?! But we were all safe in the building, watching the strong storm outside. A few minutes later, he came back and said it got a little crazy, but was all good.

The guys wouldn't let us leave until the storm passed, so we hung out in the shop with them, and they brought out popsicles for the kids! Finally, the storm lessened, and the service manager had us follow him as he directed us back to I80. I couldn't believe it - it was 4 hours since it broke down, and here we were back on the road! For a minute there, we had thought we might be stuck there until Monday and would miss the family camping weekend that the kids had been counting on for the last two months.

The fact that these guys went above and beyond to stay late and through the storm to help us shows that there are so many great people in this world who are willing to go out of their way for strangers! I want to take a minute to thank: Gene, Rod, Steven, and Rich of Thys Auto Group in Belle Plaine, Iowa, for their fantastic customer service!

They all recommended we stop at a Mercedes dealer to double-check the trans fluid and the belt as soon as we could. That wasn't going to happen that night since everything was closed, so we decided to head to our original campground reservation in Illinois for the night. It was about a 3-hour drive.

The GPS said we would get there at 11:30 pm. OK, we can handle that. Let's go. We drove and made it to the campground. As we pulled up to the gate, we saw a sign that said no check-ins after 8 pm. It was 11:30pm . . . Why hadn't anyone called us? Oh yeah, that's right, Craig's phone wasn't working.

Our RV was pretty small, so we looked over at the exit and figured I could lift the bar slightly and Craig could squeeze in. I mean, we had a reservation.

We got in, but have never been to this campground before; we had no idea where to go. We found an open campsite and pulled in, but I just didn't feel comfortable and didn't want the police waking us up in the morning asking what we were doing there!

So, we left and headed to a Walmart that was about 2 miles away to spend the night. We returned to the campground the next day to do the things we needed to do before heading to the family camping weekend. They understood the mix-up, so we were all good. And guess what? The site we had pulled into was the site we were supposed to be in that night - go figure!

What a fiasco!! Our kids did an awesome job through the whole thing. Even though everyone was covered in sweat, we had no idea where the night would lead us. What we continue to learn through these situations is we will figure it out, and there are amazing and helpful people in the world!!

After the fact, I wish I would have gotten some pictures of the whole experience, but there was just too much going on during it. And so our Crazy Family Adventure continues!

This is the reality of life on the road; things will go wrong; they just do. The key is how you handle it. It is always good to be prepared with memberships like Good Sam Roadside Assistance and to have things like an extra tire.

Besides that, these are great experiences to teach your kids how to handle unexpected situations—most of them scary and uncertain. But you can show your kids how to work together, troubleshoot together, and find a solution.

In our first year of travel, I will say we didn't have any significant issues - which was nice! Maybe that will be you, and it will be all good. If it doesn't, know you aren't alone. We have all been there!

What about doctor and dentist visits while on the road? You can totally make it work! More on that in the next chapter.

Chapter 17

Doctor And Dentist Visits

With kids, there are things like doctor visits, dentist visits, eye appointments, etc. It does present a challenge, but with a little work, it can be managed.

In our case, we have gone back to our hometown and domicile state usually once a year. We have not changed our home state, so our insurance is still there. When we do this, we always make the kids' yearly doctor and dentist appointments. Ideally, we would like this to be once a year for the doctor visits - but sometimes that ends up being spread out more like 18 months between appointments.

We do try to get them to a dentist every six months, and since we don't have dental insurance, we can use dentists wherever we are.

The main thing here is flexibility. Don't stress if you are a few months past your year mark from the last Doctor checkup. Just get in as soon as you can.

We have also found that having a service like Teledoc is excellent. In this case, you pay a one-time yearly fee - generally under $200. Then you can video chat with a doctor to ask them questions. They are also able to fill prescriptions for you.

A few years back, we went through a skin infection that almost everyone in our family got. It started with us going to a local clinic, with a set fee to have the infection examined and diagnosed. That was when we were in Destin, Florida.

The Doctor at the clinic prescribed an antibiotic to treat it. We went to the local Walgreens and picked it up. Our prescription coverage is nationwide, which helps (even though our health insurance is not - go figure)! We started treating the infection and went on our way.

Then Cannon got attacked by fire ants which bit him in his leg where the infection was. The venom from the ants canceled out the antibiotic, which we didn't realize.The infection not improving led us to a doctor in Alabama, where we were now staying. He prescribed another antibiotic to try. From there, we went on our way up to Tennessee.

By the time we got there, the infection had spread from 2 kids to 3, and I also picked it up. This time we were able to use Teledoc. We could do a video call, share what we had been experiencing, and they sent our prescription to where we were in Tennessee.

We continued to take the antibiotic and continued with our trip from Tennessee up to Winnipeg, Canada! Well, right after we crossed over the border, we started to notice that the prescription wasn't working - what the heck?!

Now that we were in Canada - Teledoc wouldn't work, so instead, we went to a local walk-in clinic in Canada. We talked to the Doctor, and she filled our prescription and told us we needed to hard-core disinfect our whole RV. Not just a little wipe down, but full-on bleach on all surfaces and wash EVERYTHING.

We were concerned about how much the prescription would cost in Canada since we knew the US one was $300 without insurance. In Canada, even without insurance, it was only $30!!! Thank goodness!!

Our first stop in Canada became the walk-in clinic and then the laundromat where we washed ALL of our clothes, chair coverings, anything we could take out of the RV. It was great spending a full day at the laundromat . . .

We ended up tossing out all of our pillows and blankets and just buying new ones. We took everything out of the RV and triple wiped everything down with bleach (usually, we try to use natural cleaners, but not in this case). The people at the RV park had to be wondering what the heck these Americans were up to?! Finally, after doing all of this, our infections started to clear, and a few weeks into our trip to Canada, we were all good! Luckily, Carson and Craig never got it.

That was an adventure that covered multiple states and countries! But we figured it out. That is a lot of what this lifestyle is about.

We have had multiple dental "emergencies" where the kids have had an abscess or I have had a filling fall out, or they have had a cavity. And in every case, we just found a local dentist, read the online reviews and went for our visit. I can't even remember the number of dentists we have visited around the US.

If you are used to going to the same doctor or dentist all your life before launching, this can be very uncomfortable. But like so many things in this lifestyle, you get used to it.

Up next we talk about sports, activities and how all of that works on the road!

Chapter 18

Sports And Activities

This is a tough one. Both Craig and I grew up playing tons of organized sports, and I went to college on a soccer scholarship, so organized sports were a big part of our childhood.

Being on the road, it isn't easy to find this unless you plan to stay put for months to participate in a season, which people do. If you don't want to do that, you will have to make a choice to not have your kids involved in these organized activities and be OK with it.

In our case, we always try to get our kids in classes - a lot of the time, they are just private lessons - whenever we are at a place for a month or more. This week we're heading to Texas to stay for one month, and we already have surf lessons lined up for 2 of the kids, and are working on getting a few other classes set up.

The key is to make sure you get it set up before you get there. A month may seem like a lot of time, but it goes fast!

We also put together our own organized football games whenever we can. This doesn't happen as much as we would like, but we want to make it more of a focus. Last winter in Florida, the kids would organize their own football games, and it was so fun to watch!

No, this isn't the same as super competitive organized sports, but it allows them to get the idea of team sports and how all of this works.

When we were in Georgia for a month, we signed Melia up for one-on-one ballet lessons and talked to the teacher about putting together a recital of sorts. So Melia learned the dance in her class and at the end we all came to watch! We even ordered her a costume on Amazon - similar to what you would do in a regular dance class.

She also did a class with her cousin. You pay more for private lessons, but you also have more control over the times you can meet and how the class works.

We have done the same for guitar lessons for the kids. We signed them up for a four-on- one class. None of them took to it - but it was the exposure piece we felt was necessary.

I still worry about this, and wonder if we are taking something away from our kids by not giving them the organized sports opportunities that both Craig and I had. My Dad was one of my coaches growing up and also had a childhood filled with sports. So, I asked him what he thought? Did he feel we were doing our kids a disservice by not having them involved in organized sports?

Since my parents also travel full-time and have been with us a lot, they see our kids and know how their days are going.

His response surprised me. He said, "No, not at all." He felt the childhood they were having was much more rewarding. It felt like a weight was lifted off my shoulders with his response - and I know it was a real answer - since he wouldn't hold back telling me the truth.

I have to say this is still something that bothers me, and sometimes I stay up at night stressing that we didn't give our kids a "normal" childhood and that they are going to wish we did. I don't have an answer for this - or think anyone does. We also continually evaluate everything, and if we feel things need to change, we will change them. When it comes to organized sports, our kids aren't asking for it. They don't seem to miss it, so we'll keep doing what we are doing.

Up next is Holiday's on the road. How does that work? What does that look like?

Chapter 19

Holidays On The Road

Holidays on the road are all up to you. Do you want to go back "home" for the holidays? Then go! Do you want to stay with just your family or find a group of friends to do the holidays with, then do that!

Holidays are one of those things that become freeing on the road. No obligation to have to go to every family party . . . instead you can choose to do the holidays exactly how you want. And if that means going home to all the family parties, then do it!

We have friends on the road who have never gone back home for the holidays. It was just too stressful of a time, and they didn't want to be part of that. Now their kids are used to spending holidays wherever they are.

We have done a few Christmases back home and a few out on the road. Each of them was good in its own way. But it can still be just as magical!

On holidays like Halloween, we are rarely ever back home, instead, we find things to do at places we visit, and our kids have never missed a year of trick-or-treating. We have trick-or-treated in Arizona in our friend's neighborhood and near Orlando in the famous Disney town, Celebration (where a lot of the Disney workers live). We made our own trick-or-treating neighborhood out on the Sand Flats in Utah while we were boondocking.

You can make it work anywhere you are with a bit of planning and research.

On the 4th of July we have seen fireworks in Colorado, Jackson Hole and back in our hometown. There are some pretty epic 4th of July events all over the country.

So don't stress about the holidays.Instead, focus more on what everyone in your immediate family wants to do!

Up next we will talk about having pets on the road and how to make it work!

Chapter 20

Pets On The Road

If you want to bring your pets with you on your travels, there is no better way than traveling in an RV. Your pets will feel right at home, and you will feel better knowing they are with you and not at someone else's house or a kennel, or being left at home for hours in between people stopping in to check on them.

We traveled full-time with our two large labrador retrievers, Indy and Odin, for four years and Indy for three years more after Odin passed away. When we first started, we had many concerns about traveling with pets, but we figured out a lot over the years! Here are our recommendations.

RV Parks

Most RV parks allow pets, but be aware that not all do, and others have limitations. Limitations you may come across are:

- Pets have to be under a certain weight.
- You can only have one pet.
- The combined weight of your dogs has to be under a certain weight.
- Certain breeds aren't allowed - Pit Bulls, Rottweilers, German Shepards, etc.

It is always good to ask what the pet rules are when you are making reservations since you don't want to show up and then not be allowed to stay! Many RV parks that allow dogs will have a dog park, which is excellent for letting your dogs off-leash for a while.

All the state and national parks we have been to allow pets to stay in the RV park/campground, but you should always double-check. They may ask for documentation showing that your pet has been vaccinated, so here are the forms that you should bring with you when traveling with your pet.

Forms To Have When Traveling With Your Pet

- Proof of vaccinations, especially rabies. You should be able to get a printed copy of this from your vet, and I would recommend also having them email it to you, so you have an electronic copy.
- Vet records. It is also good to have your vet records on hand. This isn't really for the RV park as much as it is for you to have if there is an emergency and you have to make an unexpected visit to a vet while you are traveling. It will be beneficial for the vet, who has never seen your pet before, to know the history.
- Tags. Your pet should always wear a collar with their name, your mobile number, and a rabies tag. We only take their collars off at night, but make sure to put them right back on in the morning. Even if you don't think they will ever get out, it is still good to have their collar on as often as possible. Just in case they see a stray squirrel and make a run for it out of your RV door!
- Chip information. If your pet has a chip implanted in them, make sure to have the chip number and website. Verify all information is current on your pet as well as your contact information before you leave on your trip.

Pet Food

If your pet eats a particular type of food that is only found at your local pet shop, be sure to ask them if there is anywhere else you can get it or if they could ship it to you. However, I wouldn't recommend this unless they can guarantee quick shipping or if you are planning on staying in one RV park for two weeks or more.

If you plan extended travel, you may want to switch to a dog food brand that you can find at large chain stores across the country.

Traveling in an RV, you have storage areas under your RV, but these areas are not always that large. If you want to bring all of your pet's food with you on your trip, make sure to consider storage space when buying or renting an RV. Those pet food bags can be large and heavy!

Leaving Your Pet In the RV When You Go Out

There will most likely be places you want to explore on your trip where you either don't want to bring your pet or they aren't allowed. No worries! They can stay in the RV when you are gone, but there are a few things to consider:

If it is going to be hot, you will want to run the air-conditioning and also keep some windows open in case the power goes out at the park. An RV is like a car, so if the power goes out and there is no AC, it will get HOT in your RV.

If you are worried about rain or someone climbing through a window, you can also buy rain covers for your roof vents and run the overhead fans.

If you plan on leaving your pet in your RV be sure that you are staying at an RV park with workers or security that are active during the day in case anything happens.

You should either buy or make a sign to hang by your door that tells people there are pets in the RV and leave your phone number in case of fire or a problem. Be sure to note what kind of pet you have and how many, so it is clear to any responders.

If your dog is a barker, you will need to do something about this. Having a neighbor with a barking dog is NOT fun. One of our dogs would bark when she heard a noise outside the RV if we were not inside with her. We bought a collar that spritzed a citronella mist when she barked. It took one bark for her to realize she didn't like that smell. You can pick them up at pet stores.

If you take these precautions, your pet will be fine hanging out while you go out to explore. We didn't like to do it, but if we visited somewhere a few hours from our campground, we were able to leave our dogs alone for 12 hours. We were never gone longer than that.

If you are staying at a campground that has a lot of seasonal RVers (people who come back every year and stay for four months or more), you may be able to find someone who will stop in, check on your pet or even take your dog for a walk for a fee. Your comfort level concerning a stranger entering your RV would determine if this would work for you.

Vaccines/Preventative Medicine

Of course, you will want to be sure that your dog is up to date on their vet visits and vaccines before traveling. However, you also want to be sure they are up to date on their flea, tick and heartworm medicine.

It never hurts to explain to your vet where you will be headed to see if they have any additional vaccines they would recommend. We took our pets to Colorado, and our vet recommended a Lyme Disease vaccine.

Further, you can always call a vet where you are visiting to see what they recommend for their patients. For example, in South Florida, fleas are resistant to many flea medicines that people give their pets in the northern part of the US.

And remember, just like with people, certain medicines are available over the counter, and some require a prescription. And some medications can only be prescribed after a vet has seen your pet. Again, please discuss your plans with your vet and get their recommendations about what you should bring with you.

We liked to keep a supply of:

- Heartworm medicine
- Flea/Tick medicine
- Ear infection medicine
- Upset stomach medicine

Having these on hand meant we could stay on top of preventive medicine and be prepared for unforeseen situations without having to visit a vet.

Places to Visit

If you want, you can plan your trip around places that allow dogs to participate in activities and tours and even take them out to eat with you. Below we share some of our favorite pet-friendly locations. They're part of your family, so it's always cool to include them in your vacations!

Or you can plan based on things you want to see and then find something for your pet to do when you get there. Most cities we have visited have a dog park or a local park we could go to, but don't count on all locations being inviting to dogs.

Some cities have a LOT more restrictions than others. If you are someone who wants your dog to come with you more often than not, then do some research, so you aren't disappointed.

Hotel Stays

If you think you will also include some hotel stays in your travel with your pet, you can. We have stayed at a few hotels with our dogs, and one chain that typically allows pets is La Quinta.

However, we were surprised by some of the more upper-end hotels that did, too. Be prepared; there may be a large additional fee for your pet or a limit on the number of pets or their weight. Always call ahead to ask.

Boarding Your Pet If You Are Planning To Be Away From Your RV Overnight

There were a few times we had to board our dogs. Whenever possible, we had family or friends check on and help out with our dogs.

When that wasn't an option, we learned that a person who watched dogs out of their home was our best bet. Our #1 recommendation for finding a place to leave your pet is to stop in at the local pet food/bakery. Not one of the chain stores, but more the boutique type of locally-owned shop. Talk to the owner and see who they recommend. This worked out well for us.

If that is not an option, make sure you read a LOT of reviews on kennels. If possible, bring your dog in to visit to see how they react and so you can get a feel for the place and the staff. Use your gut instinct here.

We found this site to be helpful when planning travel with our pets: http://www.bringfido.com.

RVing is the way to go if you have pets and want to do extended travel or just like the idea of having them with you. In the end, what it comes down to is that you and your pet will love the fact that you get to hang out together at night and in the morning. And, I am sure, multiple times you will sit under your awning by the picnic table together enjoying the outdoors!

Our Favorite Dog-Friendly Places

We were pleasantly surprised by how many dog-friendly places there were! In Greenfield, South Carolina, dogs were sitting by the owners outside of almost every restaurant we walked by. Then we walked by a couple, each with a snake draped around their neck! Right, they weren't dogs, but if you accept snakes, then definitely dogs will be welcome!

For someone who came from a dog-friendly city, I was surprised how not-so-dog-friendly some places were. Since traveling, a few locations stood out to us as being extra pet and specifically dog-friendly.

The Florida Keys

The majority of Florida was strict about dogs being on the beach, but once you crossed into the Florida Keys, it seemed like they were allowed almost anywhere! It might have to do with the overall vibe of the keys. But in any case, for dog lovers, it was a great location, and you felt comfortable bringing your dog with you. Oh, and hey, it was the Florida Keys!

St. Augustine, Florida

Their visitor's center had a pet-friendly document that explained all the great things you could do with your dog. The one that won us over was being able to take our dog to the Fountain of Youth!

Yup, both our dogs were able to drink water straight from the Fountain of Youth! Well, they used cups, they're not animals! If only it meant they would live forever!

Jackson Hole, Wyoming

There were multiple restaurants where pets could be with you, and they were welcome at squares/park areas throughout the town.

You also got that vibe that it was totally fine for you to have your dog with you wherever you went, and it was normal.

Another favorite spot was Slide Lake by the Grand Tetons, where the dogs could come, spend the day with us - off-leash - and swim in the lake. We all had a great time!

Colorado (pretty much the whole state is dog-friendly)

Pre-kids, Craig and I took the dogs and camped around Colorado for a week. They had boutique dog treat stores all over the place, plus some great hiking trails you could do with your dogs. But be aware, there were also trails where dogs were not recommended due to the chance of encountering a wild animal. We happily agreed to follow those recommendations and did not take those trails with our dogs.

Fort Myers Beach

As I mentioned, Florida wasn't very dog friendly when it came to beaches, but Fort Meyers had a lovely dog beach, and the water was the perfect depth so the dogs could walk in for a long way out before swimming. Plus, there were a lot of other dogs there, and everyone was totally fine with your dog being off-leash.

Jekyll Island

Pets were allowed to walk with you all around the historic district and on the many bike trails. And one of our favorite places was Driftwood beach. If you are looking for a relaxing time with your pet, I would look into Jekyll Island.

I think more and more cities are going pet-friendly, and the best tool you have for checking this when you get somewhere is Google. Google "Things to do with dogs in (whatever city you want)." There are usually going to be a lot of recommendations that come up.

We also like the site: http://www.bringfido.com. It has hotels, attractions, etc., that allow dogs. We highly recommend using this site if you are looking to plan a trip where you want to bring your dog with you wherever you go.

If you aren't sure if your pet is welcome at an attraction or restaurant, it is always good to call ahead of time to find out. Neither you nor your dog will be happy if you get somewhere and you are turned away.

Unfortunately, when our dogs got older, and our yellow lab had hip problems, we didn't take them out exploring with us as often as we would've liked. But for their sake, we felt they were more comfortable back in the RV while still enjoying getting out to go for walks or to dog parks at the RV parks/campgrounds we were at.

Traveling with your pet can add a whole other element to your trip. It can be more challenging, but it can also be fantastic to have your furry family member there with you for your adventure!

What About When Your Dog's Life Ends On The Road?

This is one of those things you never want to think about. But the reality is it can happen. In our case, both of our dogs got older, and their health went downhill, where we had to decide to bring them to the vet to be euthanized.

In both cases, we were able to take them to a place that offered cremation for dogs. I could not have imagined losing them and then just leaving them there or burying them somewhere random. It was nice we had this option to get them cremated so we could bring their ashes with us, and dispose of them in a place that we wanted to.

Needing to Go to the Vet

Going to a vet you don't know or who doesn't know your dog can be hard. Most of the time, when we had to do it, it went well, and we were happy with the service.

We would always do Google research and read the reviews to ensure we were going to the best vet in the area.
210

All in all, our take on RVing with pets is this:

If you have a dog or cat before you hit the road, bring them with you. They are part of your family, and you will figure it out.

If you don't have a dog or a cat, I wouldn't recommend getting one while you are on the road unless you plan to travel in a way that works well for the animals. I know some people can do this because they don't want to do a lot of exploring, so it can work out.

Usually families are looking to go out and see a lot and do a lot, and with a pet back home, it does make it more stressful. It is doable, but it is stressful.

Chapter 21

Keeping Things Simplified

When you live in such a small space with your family, it is imperative to keep things simplified and organized. It just makes everything easier. These are our tips on how to do that.

Plates, Bowls, Cups, Silverware

We only need one plate, one bowl, 2 cups, and two silverware sets for each person you have in your home. When we emptied our kitchen, we were amazed that we had accumulated over 40 cups of all different sizes. Most of them had dust all over them.

Lesson learned. We didn't need all of the extras. Yes, there may be times when you entertain or have people over, but you can buy paper plates, cups, etc. If you entertain a lot and don't want to buy disposable, put a small bin together with extras that you only take out and use when you need it. Or better, yet, ask people to bring their own when they come over.

This has simplified the number of dirty dishes that we have. Plus, it has trained us to wash everything right after we use it or when we need one since we don't have a whole other stack of clean ones to grab from.

Water Bottles

All 6 of us have our own water bottle, and it is the bottle we drink out of when we are at home or if we are out and about. So again, we don't need a ton of glasses during the day because everyone has their water bottle that they use.

Plus, since we mainly just drink water, we keep the water bottles filled all day, and are good to go.

Clothes

We all had WAY too many clothes back in our house. We had clothes collecting dust that we hadn't worn in years, but just kept shoving to the back of the closet. Moving into a small space made us do a deep clean out of our clothes, and to be honest, there has not been one thing I have gotten rid of that I wish I hadn't.

Our wardrobe is quite basic since we don't have to go to work. It is pretty much beach-bum vacation kind of clothes. If we were to stay in a cold climate, we might have to buy a few things, but I think we would be fine for the most part.

For us, it comes down to about four pairs of shorts, ten shirts, five tank tops, four pairs of pants, five long sleeve shirts, a few nicer outfits, a couple of sweatshirts, swimsuits, and that is about it. Those numbers aren't exact for each person in our family, but you get the idea. We don't have a lot, but it works.

We have a washer/dryer in our RV, so if I stay on top of it and wash clothes everyday or every other day, there are plenty of clothes for all of us. We do wear the same clothes more than once without washing, if at all possible.

When we have had rigs without a washer and dryer, we would find a local laundromat and do laundry about once a week.

The kids may go 2 or 3 days in the same clothes, assuming they haven't gotten them covered in mud or sand. They will also wear their clothes for the next day to bed at night. They don't wear pajamas. It saves the hassle of having to fight them to change in the morning and saves us room!

If you are a shoe lover or love the idea of planning cute and different outfits every day, this may be a stretch for you, but I think you could get a system in place that works!

Cooking

When we moved into the RV, we went through all of our cooking items and narrowed them down to only the things we used consistently. This did mean we kept the donut maker since we use it a lot. But we got rid of the huge Wok and the toaster oven we'd never used.

We also got rid of our pots and pans and replaced them with two cast-iron pieces. We have a cast-iron skillet and a dutch oven. There have been only a handful of times where we wished we had something more than that.

We also have some baking pans, a mixing bowl, muffin tins, a blender, toaster, etc. It's just the bare minimum that we use pretty consistently. It really simplifies our whole kitchen only to have the pieces that we use regularly.

Eating

Our eating is very simple. We don't do large elaborate meals. We do simplified meals with just a handful of ingredients. And we repeat those same meals week after week. This doesn't mean they aren't healthy. We try our best to avoid too many processed foods.

It Never Ends

We are always working on simplifying our lives. Just last week, we donated four big garbage bags full of stuff. It felt so good to free up more space. We go through everything with the kids and decide together what we should keep and what we should donate. It's a process, but our kids are getting better at letting go of things they no longer need or play with.

Of course, it never ends because we still accumulate things. Not at the rate we did when we were in a house, but we still get stuff now and then. Our twins recently had birthdays, and with Christmas a couple of months ago, we added quite a few toys to the mix.

Helping Kids Agree To A Simplified Lifestyle

Sometimes someone wants something big like a gymnastics beam, which we were able to do by finding a foldable one. But it is an ongoing conversation to help them see why we shouldn't always buy more. It means Mommy and Daddy can work less, there is less cleaning and we have more space. And it has been amazing to watch them accept it and embrace it.

I will be interested to see if they keep their lives simplified as adults, or if they will be people who go out and buy a lot of things. At this point, we feel we are showing them a lifestyle that could work for them as adults, while also showing them why we are choosing to live this way.

In Conclusion

It comes down to us having one and, if possible, only one of the things we need per person. One towel, one sweatshirt, one pair of sunglasses, one backpack, one water bottle, etc. We all have two to three pairs of shoes, but are very conscious of not getting more than that.

It isn't always easy to keep things simplified, but the more we do it, the easier it gets, and we feel like we are going in the right direction for our family. It has also gotten easier to walk through Target and Walmart and not pick up fifteen extra things! I have it down to about five and hope to be at zero soon!

Keeping our life simplified allows us to focus more on each other rather than our things. And having a lot of stuff requires a lot of energy. Simplifying works for us, and we will keep pushing ourselves to simplify more and more.

The longer we are on the road the more we have been pushing the boundaries a bit . . . and getting some fun toys like a Blackstone grill, paddleboards, kayaks, etc. But whenever we start to get too much again, we begin to feel like we need to do a major purge!

Living simplified can be very addicting. Once you see how nice it is, you want to keep it that way. But even feeling this way, it is crazy how materialistic things still sneak back in. It is a balancing act, and we are continually working at it!

In the next chapter we share a variety of different travel styles that we have seen while being on the road. This really was a surprise to us as we thought everyone would be doing the same thing. But they aren't!

Chapter 22

Travel Style

When we first decided to travel full-time in our RV with our family of 6, we figured everyone we met would be just like us, travel like us, eat like us, school like us, drink like us, well, you get the picture.

We quickly learned that there are many different reasons why families hit the road and how they live life on the road. It is fascinating! Here are some of the different styles we have observed:

Stationary

One option is to move into an RV and then stay at one location full-time. You don't ever move your RV/Trailer/5th Wheel, but instead, it stays at the campground. Families may do this if they find a location they love, enjoy living in campgrounds for the community or are looking to save money. Whatever their reason, they plan to stay put for a longer stretch (potentially a year or more).

Apartment On Wheels

Another option is to buy the biggest RV/Trailer/5th Wheel you can find. And honestly, they look like an apartment or condo inside! Some have multiple bedrooms, a balcony, a garage. There are some pretty sweet setups out there.

We have found that families with apartments on wheels still do a lot of traveling and may travel every 1 - 3 weeks to a new location. There can be a few challenges getting a rig that big into a campsite. But once in there and settled, having that apartment on wheels can be pretty darn sweet!

Structured

This one was a surprise to us. We thought everyone we met would be as unstructured as we are. Not even close! Instead, most of the families we have met try to stay on a pretty strict school, bedtime, and daily routine with their families. It's like they have taken their life from their sticks and bricks and just moved it into an RV/Trailer/5th Wheel.

9 to 5er

We started this way. Craig was working a regular 9 to 5 job, but he could do it remotely. So that meant he worked Monday - Friday during the day. Then at night or on the weekends, we would go out to do things as a family. And our travel day was always on a weekend so he could work on Monday.

A lot of the families on the road have taken this approach. The nice thing about it for us was the stability of income, insurance, and work schedule. There is something to be said for that. You work all week, but then every weekend is a vacation in a new location.

Traveler

These people have a plan to go and see it all as fast as they can. Usually, they have a set time they will be on the road, so they try to get it all in and don't want to miss anything.

Boondocker

This is the option where you try to push the system and see how many nights you can stay for FREE at boondocking places around the country. There are some pretty unique RV setups out there with solar, composite toilets, higher clearance wheels, etc. They are awesome!

Usually, if you are a boondocker, you aren't looking for that campsite vibe and try to avoid them as much as possible.

Thousand Trails Traveler

Thousand Trails is a membership campground where once you buy the membership and pay your yearly fee, you can stay for free at their campgrounds all over the country. We didn't know about this when we started, but quickly met many families that were members and ended up getting a membership.

This group of travelers are the families that move from one Thousand Trails to another (you can stay up to 3 weeks at a time unless you have an annual site). This is a very cost-effective way to get out and see the country with low camping fees and full hookups - unlike the boondockers.

Entrepreneurs

I am surprised that we haven't met more entrepreneurs on the road. These are the families where one or both parents are running their own business from the road. We now fall into this category.

Retired Military

We were also surprised how many retired military families we have met on the road. In these families one of the parents is retired and getting a pension, which they can use to live and travel. Almost all the families I have met, though, one or both parents are doing some work to bring in more income.

Airstreams

We did not know that people with Airstreams had their Airstream groups. Don't get me wrong; they are always very inviting to anyone who wants to join them to hang out or camp with them. I just know you don't get to do the Airstream head nod if you pull up with your Class C! Honestly, though, I think it is fantastic that they have Airstream rallies where they can talk about their rigs and get ideas. They are pretty sweet!

Unschoolers

When we were thinking about hitting the road, we already knew we were going to Unschool, and to be honest, I thought a lot of the other people we met on the road would be Unschooling, too. That has not been the case. Instead, there have been times I have said we Unschool and people look at me like it is a dirty word.

Most RVers homeschool their kids, but they are usually following a curriculum, doing online school, or roadschooling in a structured format. I think it is great that each family figures out what works for them, and I know that Unschooling isn't for everyone.

Who would have thought there were so many different styles and ways to travel full-time with your family? But I love that when you meet up with other families at a campground, the kids could care less about how they are traveling. They just want to get together to run and play!

We have sat around fires and hung out with a variety of people and travelers, and it is such a cool part of this lifestyle. We get to interact and learn from families and people we probably never would have met if we'd stayed in our sticks and bricks.

And even if you don't agree on everything, everyone has something to offer!

The Difference Between Vacation and Full-time Travel

When following our social media accounts, it may look like we are on vacation every day. And there are days and times it feels like that. But not always. Full-time family travel is not a full-time family vacation.

Full-time family travel is a lifestyle. This is how we live. We still do all the usual things we would do living in a house like watch TV, do art projects, just hang out, etc. We still go to the doctor and the dentist. And we have to go grocery shopping and prepare meals on a budget.

When we were preparing to hit the road, I remember how excited I was about this continuous adventure, and it is precisely that! But I was also concerned about what downtime would look like. How would this work? It is an ever-evolving process, but we are figuring it out.

When we first get somewhere, I want to run out and go and see and do everything! I want to be on vacation. It always takes me a minute to stop myself and remember this is our life, not a vacation.

On vacation, we were usually at a location for a short time, so we could only do the highlights or hit the top tourist destination. Now that we travel full-time, we can stay at a place for a month or two and dive into the location and find out what the locals do. Or we can do the same thing multiple times and experience it at a deeper level.

We love this part of full-time travel. We see the weekenders come and go, and we are happy that we don't have to leave yet. We see people running from attraction to attraction, and we appreciate that we don't have to do that.

On vacation, we would buy souvenirs, go out to eat, and splurge on activities and shows. With full-time travel, we still want to do those things, but we have to remember that this is our life and we are going to be on another "vacation" next week or month, so we have to keep a handle on our splurges since we just can't afford to vacation every week!

This can be tough when every attraction we go to has us walk through a gift shop on the way out! Craig and I and the kids have gotten used to the idea that we don't stop in the gift shops. We just keep walking through.

We have to work. This can be a tough one. We are at these fantastic places, and we just want to get out and see everything, explore, and immerse ourselves in the location. But we need money to live, so we have to find time to work. On vacation, you can hopefully leave your worries behind and shut down your phone or computer and disconnect. I know not everyone does that on vacation, but I know that was what we used to do before we started traveling full-time.

Finding the balance between exploring, traveling and working has been a challenge. Yes, we can still set up times when we vacation where we don't work. But we can't do that 365 days out of the year.

Constant Planning. Planning for a vacation is fun - you can't wait to go, so you spend lots of time looking into the location and figuring out what you will do. When you travel full-time, it feels like you are doing that planning every other day. When we visit a new location every 3 to 4 weeks, that is a lot of planning! It gets old. Or it gets stressful because we worry that we are going to miss something. Between raising kids, working and exploring our current location, there is barely any time to plan for the next place. It becomes another "job" and starts to become something we don't look forward to.

Enjoying the Lifestyle and Not Just the Destinations

One of the things I have loved is how we have adapted to not just enjoying where we are going but also enjoying the lifestyle. Having slow days or even weeks is all about hanging out with each other or the friends we are traveling with.

It's about cooking meals with other families, sitting around the campfire, just hanging out, and not worrying about being everywhere and seeing everything.

I understand if you are only doing this for a year, you may feel the pressure to go and see and do everything. But I would also challenge you to find joy in the simple parts of this lifestyle and make those a priority.

If you get to a place and find another family you and your kids connect with, change your plans. Cancel that next reservation and extend your stay to enjoy time relaxing and letting the kids just play while you all get to know the new family you met.

The connections you make on the road can be amazing, if you give yourself time to find them and enjoy them!

I love that there are so many different ways to do this lifestyle, and each of them is awesome in its own way. Also, I think you can jump between these different styles while you are on the road and experience a variety of them.

This leads to talking about planning. How do you plan where you are going to go next? What are you going to see and do? Where are you going to stay? So many things to figure out!

Chapter 23

Planning

Okay, you're ready to hit the road! Now you have to figure out where you are going to stay EVERY SINGLE NIGHT!

There is a whole lot of planning that goes into this style of living. It isn't like having a house that you know you can go back to every night. Instead you have to be sure you have a campsite booked or somewhere in mind to stay for the night - each and every night!

This takes work and planning. Yes, it gets easier after a while, but it is always there.

Also, know there are campgrounds that can be completely booked up 6-12 months in advance. This is especially true of National Park campgrounds. Yes, you read that right. If you really want to stay IN Yellowstone National Park (which we do highly recommend) then you are going to have to get your spot booked way in advance or take a chance on a first come first serve spot or cancellation.

There are definitely different ways you can do this lifestyle when it comes to figuring out where you will go.

Non-Planners

You will meet some non-planners who don't even know where they are staying tonight. But given that they choose to live this way they always figure it out. Even if it means staying in a Walmart parking lot or a rest area for some hours. These people will tell you this is the best way to travel because you are always available if a new opportunity comes up. And a lot of the time you end up in places that are really cool - which you would have missed if your whole month had been booked at RV parks and campgrounds.

Yes, there are benefits to being a non-planner. But that also means you have to be able to live this way. Not everyone can. But if this is what you desire, you can definitely work at it!

If you want to go this route, I recommend you have all of the RV apps (covered in Chapter 8) on your phone, are active in a variety of RVing Facebook groups and are good at looking for and finding lots of different options for overnight stays.

The Plan A, Plan B and Plan C Planner

These people don't want to commit to one place, but do want to have options so they know they have a place for the night. They may have multiple reservations for any given time. Then once they decide where they want to go, they just cancel the other reservations. Yes, sometimes there is a $15 - $20 fee to cancel but they're OK with that since they like this flexibility.

The Planner

Then there are others who literally have their whole year planned out and booked. These people always blow my mind. We rarely know where we will be next month and here they have their whole year planned out!

There is a part of me that likes the idea of it all being done. Then, again, I think having all those commitments would stress me out!

In any case, there is no right way to do the planning. It is about how you want to plan.

Planning for the Busy and Cold months while full-time RVing.

Summer:

In the Summer, when kids are out of school, there are a lot of people traveling. This means places book up and they book up early (again, like 6-12 months in advance). So keep that in mind when looking at summer travel.

We have found that weekdays tend to be more open, but weekends are very difficult for getting last minute campgrounds. You may be able to find one but they will probably be a lot more expensive or not exactly what you are looking for.

Holidays:

Holidays usually means more people are camping. Labor Day, Memorial Day, Presidents Day, etc. When you aren't on a school schedule you can easily forget about these holidays. They can sneak up on you and you won't have anything booked!

This has happened to us a few times. We always found somewhere but it may not have been exactly where we wanted to be. Now I try to make sure we have spots for all the holidays a few months in advance - or plan to boondock during those times.

Winter:

This came as a surprise to me. Being from Wisconsin, I just assumed most places down south were warm all winter! Not the case. If you are looking for warm swimming weather with shorts and tank tops all year, your options are pretty limited.

To get that type of weather, you usually have to be south of Orlando, in the Phoenix area or Mexico. Not saying you can't stay further north, but just know that the weather is going to be cool or cold the further north you get.

This being the case, Florida and Arizona are PACKED in winter with RVers. Both families and retirees. This means that planning ahead is usually a necessity, especially if you want to get particular campgrounds.

If the Florida Keys are high on your list (which we totally recommend), know that you will want to book those State Park campgrounds 11 months out. Yes, there are private RV parks you can book closer to the date, but they are 3 times the price. There are some Trail Collections (an add- on to a Thousand Trails membership) parks down there so that may be another option, but just know some pre-planning is needed.

Now all that being said, we aren't big planners and rarely ever have more than a few months ahead planned out. What we have figured out is HOW we need to do this planning to make it work. And at times we've had to settle for not the exact site or campground that we wanted.

With a Thousand Trails membership we are able to book sites online up to 90 days out (memberships vary on this timeline) and then we can cancel them. So if we aren't 100% sure what we are doing, we may book a set of dates and then go and change or cancel them depending on our plans.

We've also kept an eye on the booking system at places and would check daily to see if anything opened up. This worked to get us into National Parks last minute a few times when people had canceled a reservation.

You have to be comfortable with uncertainty and also comfortable with the fact you may end up boondocking somewhere for a few days if nothing is available. It is up to you to decide how that works for you.

There are a lot of different ways to find good destinations.

Instagram

Instagram is filled with pictures of people showing you the best of the best places. And a lot of the time they really are that cool. So Instagram can be a great place to get ideas of places you want to visit.

You can search Instagram by hashtags or follow other RVers. When you see a place you like, you can Save it to a folder on Instagram called Cool Places. Then when you are ready to find somewhere new you can look back at the old posts.

Destination Books

I am a big one for the Moon Travel Guides. If I know we are going to be exploring a particular state for a while I like to get that state's Moon Guide. It helps me find the top places we should go and really helps with planning an itinerary once we get there.

Google

Of course, there is always Google which we use a lot. I am always searching for things to do in the location we're visiting. I also Google Top Places to visit in a specific state or top hikes, top hot springs, etc.

Word of Mouth

Talk to people. Ask them what their favorite places have been. Take notes so you don't forget. Word of mouth is a great way to find really cool and off the beaten path places.

Apps/Websites

There are some apps out there that will give you recommendations. Or you can try websites like RoadTrippers or Atlas Obscura.

Again, how you plan all comes down to your style and how you want to go about finding things to do. You will quickly figure out your style and preferences once you are on the road.

Is going on hiking trips part of your vision of life on the road?! Perfect! Up next we share tips on how to get your kids out and hiking. Power pellets are our secret weapon!

Chapter 24

Hiking With Kids

When you go on the road full-time, you will most likely want to visit a lot of National and State Parks. This usually means there will be hiking involved. If you are like us, this may be your first introduction to hiking for your family. Never fear; it is still possible to become hikers and to enjoy it with your kids!

When we started full-time traveling, we weren't a big hiking family, so it took some time to figure out how best to hike as a family. We have gone on an over 6 miles long hike with our four kids under the age of 9, and a few years later did a 15-mile hike with a 4,000-foot elevation gain to walk on a glacier.

Hiking with kids can be a fantastic time and a great way to bond as a family. Below we share 15 tips on how to make that happen:

Expectations When Hiking With Kids

This is the biggest one by far. Your expectations have to be realistic. There are going to be challenges when you are hiking with kids. Don't expect everyone to be happy all the time, and don't expect your kids to hike beyond their limit.

Get Over It

Another big one. If your kids break down while you are hiking, either from being tired, falling or just being bored, address the situation. This may mean having to stop and take a break in the middle of the trail or carrying your kid (even if they are 5, 6 or 7) for a little while.

Once the situation is addressed, get over it and move on. Don't dwell on it. Instead, be upbeat and happy and continue with the hike. Your kids will feed off of your energy, so be prepared for this one so you can bounce back quickly when things get tough.

Plan to Stop To Let the Kids Explore

I like to start and get to the end. I want to walk fast and keep moving. That doesn't always work with kids. It will make the whole experience better if you give them a chance to stop and explore now and then. Don't get me wrong, you still have to keep moving, or a 1-mile hike could take 4 hours!

If they see something they want to explore, let them stop to check it out. Just remind them that you have to keep moving to reach your destination, have your picnic or get your "Power Pellets." This would also be an excellent time to bust out a game idea to help them move again (game ideas listed below!)

Power Pellets

Oh, the Power Pellets have saved us quite a few times. These are little pellets that we give the kids and tell them they are magical energy tablets, so they get a burst of energy to keep hiking! (Shhh… they're just Tic-Tacs). They are the perfect size for giving kids, yummy, and easy to carry with you on a hike (they fit right in my fanny pack!) It makes the kids feel like they have this burst of energy when they eat them.

Sometimes I tell the kids before we start that we have them. Other times I keep it to myself, so they aren't asking the minute we start the hike. It is up to you how your kids handle that if you want to tell them upfront or not.

Suckers

If it is a longer hike, I double up. We bring the Power Pellets and suckers. Suckers work great since it takes the kids a while to eat them, and they are occupied as they are walking, so they keep moving. Ring Pops are also great since they last a long time.

Hiking Snacks For Kids

If you are hiking to an endpoint like a scenic view, lake, park, etc., it is always good to pack a few snacks for your kids. This doesn't have to be a gourmet meal, but just simple things like graham crackers, granola bars or fruit snacks.

Finding hiking snacks for kids doesn't have to be hard. Just think of things your kids like that you would pack in their lunch or are easy to take with you. You can also get the snack size zip-lock bags and make little snack bags for each kid with their favorite chips, crackers, candy (if it is hot out, you might want to steer clear of chocolate), etc.

If you have older kids, you could get them a kids-sized small pack to carry their own snacks and water. This has been helpful for our kids as they got older – they could eat their snacks when they wanted to and weren't always asking us to get them out of our bag.

You can also add things like a magnifying glass or a safety whistle (but may want to talk to the kids about only using the whistle in emergencies, or they will be blowing it the whole hike!)

Don't forget to bring a can of beer or bottle of wine so you can energize (or relax), too!

Hiking Games For Kids

There are a few hiking games for kids we have found that work well. They don't take any equipment, which makes them perfect.

Storytelling

- Ask each kid questions and from there, put a story together. For example, is the story about a boy or girl?
- What is the kid's name?
- Where are they going?
- What do they do when they get there?
- And just keep going and putting the story together as the questions are answered.

Guess the animal

- Pick an animal, and then the kids ask questions to figure out what animal you are thinking of.
- Then have your kids pick an animal, and answer the questions. We even did this when our son was only 4, and it worked great.

I Spy

- A basic game of I spy where you pick something and say "I spy something blue (or whatever color) with my little eye."and give hints until they guess it.

Scavenger Hunt

- Kids always love a good scavenger hunt!

These hiking games for kids can take a long time and keep everyone occupied and hiking while also having fun together!

Talking While Hiking With Kids

This one works great with our older son. He tends to get fixated on topics, so he will hike for hours if we talk to him about them.

Hiking with kids is a great time to really bond with them and just let them talk. On one hike, our then 6-year-old spoke for the whole 2-mile hike. Seriously, he talked the entire time. As we all know, life is busy, but when you are on a hike, there usually isn't much else you can do, so it is a perfect time just to let your kid talk and to listen. It can be fascinating what they have to say.

If your kid doesn't easily open up and talk, then be prepared with questions you can ask like:

- What was your favorite thing about yesterday?
- What is your favorite flavor of ice cream?
- What color leaves do you like best?
- What do you want to do tomorrow?
- Anything about them that they can answer without being judged or that doesn't have a right or wrong answer.

Backpack Carrier

We have used our backpack carrier even for our kids when they were six-year-olds! We used an Ergo, and yes, our kids were out of the weight limit, but they still worked for taking pressure off of our backs while we were carrying them. Sometimes, our then four-year-old would stay in it for miles, and sometimes he wanted to get down and run. It was one of our hiking essentials with young kids. Just having it with us gave everyone a chance to take a break if they needed it. Plus, it was a good workout for Mom or Dad!

Water

Don't skip this one! Your kids will get thirsty, and so will you, so have water bottles with you. Make sure you have brought as much water with you as you can carry comfortably.

Backpacks are great for this. Depending on where you are hiking and how far, be sure you are keeping an eye on water intake, so you don't drink all of it before you are even halfway done with your hike.

Shoes

Having the right hiking shoes for kids is very helpful. With the right shoes, they will not trip and fall as much, lose their shoes, or have to worry about getting them wet or dirty. Don't let them wear their best new shoes when you go hiking. Instead, get a pair of Keens or an old pair of shoes that they can get dirty and wet. Keens are great because they have excellent toe protection.

Kids love exploring, and to help them enjoy hiking, it is best to let them explore as much as possible and not worry about their shoes getting dirty or wet. If your kid doesn't like wet shoes or socks, bring an extra pair of socks or explain to them if their shoes get wet, you don't have another pair with you. This may not work the first time, but the next time around, they will understand better.

Clothes

Always have a pair of dry clothes in the car when you go hiking with kids. If possible, bring a change of clothes with you in your backpack on your hike. That way, if the kids see a stream or fall in a mud puddle, you have clothes for them to change into. This will help your kids enjoy hiking more.

If they aren't stressing about their clothes, they are bound to have more fun and explore more. This also goes for parents – always have an extra pair of clothes in the car just in case you get caught in the rain or end up playing in the stream with your kids.

If you are worried about the sun, bring a sun hat for your kid too. Especially, if you will be doing a hike out in the open.

Type of Hike

Our kids love a hike that has them climbing up and over things or going into the water. Think about the age of your kids and what kind of hike they would be into. We don't always do kid-friendly hikes – but instead, push our kids to do more challenging hikes.

Also, what can you handle? Because you have to be able to keep up. Our kids love rock scrambling (where you are climbing over rocks and up rocks to stay on the trail) and would go for miles with that kind of hike.

Have An End Destination When Hiking With Kids

A loop hike is nice since you just go out and make a loop, and you don't backtrack on the same trail. But having an end goal like a waterfall or a lookout is also really cool and can motivate the kids to keep going to reach that point.

Just make sure you make it more than just about the picture when you get there. I took the kids a mile up a mountain to Clingmans Dome lookout in the Smoky Mountains, and when we got to the top, Melia turned to me and said, "We did all of that just for a picture?!" I bought all of them something at the gift shop when we got to the bottom to make up for it.

When you reach the destination, you could set up a picnic. Or take a break to sit on a log and enjoy the scenery while snacking on something special you have been saving just for that time. Or just give them a chance to run around or jump in the water (if by a waterfall).

Above All, Enjoy Yourself!

Know that this isn't going to be like hiking with adults, and if that is what you are looking for, find a babysitter for your kids and go without them. Hiking with kids can be so fun and such a great family bonding experience, so we recommend going for it! Don't expect the first or even the 3rd or 10th time to go perfect because it probably won't, but stick with it, and you and your family will figure it out.

If you tell kids that they will have Power Pellets and candy on the hike, they will get more excited about it. I know I get more excited when I know I have a Mike's Hard Lemonade waiting for me at the end of the hike. Hiking with kids is all about doing what you have to do to make it work. Over time, it takes less and less of that, and your kids get used to it and usually enjoy it!

The biggest thing is you have to just start doing it! Get out there and go for it, and before you know it, it will be easier for everyone.

Okay, we are getting to the end of the book here, and I hope you have taken a lot away so far. Up next, I want to share our insights after being on the road after one year, two years, and three years. I have said this before and will say it again: this is a journey in more ways than you can imagine. When you read through these insights from over the years, you will see how we were evolving, and so was our journey.

Chapter 25

Year 1, 2, 3 and Beyond

This chapter will share the insights we had after each of our first 3 years of full-time RV travel. We wrote this content right after we finished each year.

Year 1

We've had quite a year traveling in an RV. We sold our house, most of our stuff and moved into an RV. We've traveled to some great places and made some great friends. Check out what we've learned about this lifestyle and ourselves in general.

We like this lifestyle!

To be honest, there were times when we weren't sure about traveling in an RV. There are still times now and then where we question this crazy choice, we've made. But it only lasts for a short time, and we are right back to being content and happy with our decision.

You don't need 75% of the stuff you think you need when you live in a house.

When we sold our 3000 square foot house, we sold almost everything we had. I could not believe how many plates, cups and wine glasses we had! Who needs 40 cups, and where did these all come from?! Not to mention all the toys, games, clothes, and everything else you fill your house with. I am sincere when I say we have not missed any of it.

Living in a small space is easier to manage.

Yes, the RV turns into a disaster when the kids are playing, or we are making dinner, etc. But it is incredible how in a matter of 30 minutes, it is all picked up. And with another 30 minutes, we could have the whole thing wiped down and cleaned, and only another 30 minutes to do a deep clean. In our house, that is the amount of time I would spend just in our kitchen cleaning. Oh, wait, that's right, our whole RV is about the size of my old kitchen . . .

We need to be in better shape!!

You know how when you go on vacation, you always come home and then feel like you need another vacation from your vacation. . . guess what, we never stop! The "vacation" just continues. It isn't all a vacation, but the whole moving process (we move like every 1 to 2 weeks), familiarizing ourselves with a new place and experiencing new things is exhausting! It is excellent, but man, we need to be in better shape to keep up with this lifestyle, our dogs, and our kids!

It isn't all fun and games.

There is a lot of stress involved in full-time RVing and not knowing where we will be staying the next month. You can't just say, oh, I will wait and figure that out later. If you do that, you may not have somewhere to stay. So you have to plan! You know the saying: It is nice to know someone who has a boat that you can visit, since they have so many issues and are hard to maintain. Well, it is the same thing with an RV. There is always something that needs to be fixed or looked at.

Yes, I know a house is the same way. But this is just another reason why this isn't always a vacation – we aren't visiting a hotel where someone takes care of everything. We have to maintain where we live. And guess what? If the RV doesn't work, we have a problem! We have to move to the next place, so we have to be sure it works. Also, I took our local grocery store so for granted! Do you know how hard it is to have to shop in a new grocery store almost every week? Let me tell you; it is a challenge!

We aren't on vacation.

This is a hard one to adjust to since it sure does seem like you are on vacation. I mean, most of the other people at the RV parks ARE on vacation. So they are having a drink and grilling out at noon on a Monday, and here we are having to work, do laundry, go grocery shopping, etc. Not to mention when you visit all these cool places you want to do everything.

But guess what, that is expensive. And I mean REALLY expensive when you have four kids. So we have had to change our mindset to not always being able to stay at the RV park we want but instead finding the best-priced one. We have to pick and choose the things we do at each place so we can afford it.

Have to love Google and being able to Google FREE things to do in a city! Plus, we have gotten some great memberships – National Park membership and the Reciprocal Museum membership.

Camping is EXPENSIVE

You think traveling in an RV sounds cheap and that there are so many expenses we don't have. Well, that is true. But have you looked up campground rates lately?! Most of them are over $40 a night for full hook-up (sewer, water, and electric). And if you want to stay at a State Park, they still average around $20 a night, which usually only includes electric hookups. We learned quickly that we didn't want to be spending thousands of dollars a month on campgrounds, so we joined Thousand Trails.

It is a membership program where we pay a one-time fee to purchase the membership and then yearly dues. After that you can stay at one of their campgrounds around the country for free for three weeks. Then you can move to another campground for three weeks and stay there for free. It's possible to find TT parks all over the country and just camp for "free" all year. This has been an excellent way for us to camp for less and to lower our monthly burn rate.

There are so many AMAZING things to see and do!!

I was never that good at geography. So it is fantastic now that when we talk about a state, I know exactly where it is and everything about what it has to offer. And every state and city truly has something to offer. We still have so many places we want to see, and we haven't even been out West yet. This is by far one of the biggest highlights of doing this. We get to SEE all those places that everyone wants to see and has on a bucket list. We are lucky that we have been able to do so!

You better LIKE your Husband and Kids.

When traveling in an RV, you spend a LOT of time together – by that, I mean 24/7, 52 weeks out of the year! Luckily for us, we do all like each other. This is not to say it is perfect because it is far from it. But I feel so lucky to be able to spend all this time with them. The bond we are building with each other is amazing, and that in itself is such a positive aspect of doing what we are doing. We all know what each other is into, how they feel, how they handle things, what they like, and don't like. We are truly immersed in each others' lives because there is nowhere to hide :).

Making friends

We did not expect to make such awesome and great friends so quickly in this lifestyle. Yes, there are more crazy people like us out there traveling in an RV, and it has been great finding them and connecting with them. You know how fun it is to spend a weekend camping with your friends? Well guess what, we have been able to do this for weeks on end. The kids are seriously getting the Endless Summer, and it is great for everyone! Not to mention all the great tips that you learn from each other, the support when things go wrong, and having help planning where you are going next and what you will be doing when you get there!

We can't believe we've already been traveling in an RV for a year! We have no end date in sight and plan to continue with this lifestyle. There are so many places we still haven't been within the US and the World!! If you have ever thought about doing something like this or have another dream you want to do – GO FOR IT!!! Stop thinking you will do it next year and do it THIS year!! I can't promise it will be easy (or the right decision), but I can promise that it will help you grow as a person and a family and will help you know what you are capable of, and will give you more clarity about what you want to do with your future.

Year 2

We have lived full-time on the road for 2 Years – WOW! We can't believe it has been that long, and yet, it feels like we have always lived this life of full-time traveling.

What has been cool about year two is that we have started to see more transformational changes in us as people, as a family, as business owners. It has been quite the journey! Year 1 was about learning how to live this way. So year two became more about choices, decisions, options, etc., around working and living full-time on the road.

Awesomeness is everywhere!

Everywhere we go – no matter how big or small of a city or town it is – offers something awesome. Sure, a little town in Alabama may not have the best (or any) farmer's market, but they have a fantastic lake with a cliff jumping area that is perfect for the kids!

The festivals, breweries and parks that we have found throughout the country (mostly east coast and midwest at this point) all brought something unique and different to the table. Maybe it was the scenery behind the festival, be it a mountain or an ocean. Or the vibes from the people that were there. Each one was familiar yet different.

Taking a boat out 70 miles to the Dry Tortugas off of Key West, Florida, was breathtaking, and so was sliding down Sliding Rock near Asheville and feeding a sloth at the zoo. It isn't about only doing the things we know we like, but trying a variety of different things and seeing the beauty and fun in all of them!

We live in a fantastic world (which we are hoping to see more of in the future), but also a pretty darn cool country! The US has such incredible landscapes and variety. We have fallen in love with the melting pot that it is, and RV traveling allows us to experience it.

Having choices is hard.

We have set up our lifestyle as a lifestyle of freedom. No set schedules or times that we need to be anywhere, and our reservations can always be changed. This is amazing, yet causes problems. Since our time is ALL ours, we could all stay in our pajamas all day, every day, if we wanted to. Of course, we don't do that because we have to work and the kids can't sit still that long.

The thing is, when we work is totally up to us. We could work starting at 6 am or not open our computer until 10 pm. It is totally up to us. We can also explore a new location or just stay back at the campground and go swimming. I know it sounds great, and it is, but it puts a lot of pressure on us to decide what we will do with our time since no one tells us what to do.

We are happy with having this "problem" and are learning how to manage it, but it was an issue that we really didn't see coming.

We are ready to downsize.

When we first thought about part-time RV living with kids, we bought a 29-foot class C motorhome without slide-outs. We thought It was the perfect RV for trips. Then when we decided to go full-time, we thought it would be too small. So we found a beautiful 39′ coach with four slide-outs and tons of basement storage. Perfect! Right??

How things change! Now we are ready to move into something smaller again. We want to sell our current rig and move into a 26 foot or smaller class C. We are getting too comfortable in our current rig, so it is time to push the comfort zone again! Having a smaller rig will also mean less money (on gas, payments, maintenance, etc.), and it means we can get in and out of places with less planning.

We are nervous and excited about what downsizing will be like.

Comfort zones are made for pushing.

Our life is all about pushing our comfort zone. Yes, we get tired of this and sometimes long for the peacefulness and comfort of what we know. But then we quickly move out of that and back into pushing ourselves to discover and explore the unknown.

We have been amazed at how every time we push our comfort zone and struggle through the fear and uncertainty, we come out on the other end better for it. We become more well-rounded as people and as parents. It has also shown us that once we push our comfort zone one time, we can do it over and over again.

We will continue to push our comfort zones, and are excited about what that means, and where that will take us as we continue to move forward and into unknown territory.

We don't like "dry" counties.

A dry county is a county that can't sell alcohol. YES, they exist in the US! Coming from Wisconsin, where there is a bar on every other corner, we were surprised that we would have to drive 45 minutes to buy beer and wine. Craig said we need an app that alerts you when you are nearing a dry county so you can stop and stock up! Patent pending.

Keens are the only shoes you need

We got a pair of Keen sandals for each of us, and they have been perfect for our lifestyle. They can get wet and can be used for hiking.

The kids don't even have running shoes anymore. They just have a pair of Keens and a pair of flip-flops or Crocs.

The only problem is they smell pretty bad after a while, but we have found that if we wash them in the washing machine, they are all good, again, for a bit!

We can REALLY annoy each other.

I mean, come on now, RV living with kids means we are together literally 24/7, so it is bound to happen! And it does. There are days when we are all at our wit's end and just don't want to be together anymore. These are usually the days when we will jump in the car and go for a ride so everyone can be in their car seat, contained and just relaxing – with the TV on and an iPad in hand. And we don't feel guilty about it!

That being said, we have also learned how to adapt to each other's moods so that the annoying point doesn't come as often. Or if Craig and I feel it coming on, we will get everyone out of the RV/campground and find a new park/playground where the kids can run the energy off.

We really like each other.

Yes, we can annoy the crap out of each other, but we also really like each other and enjoy each other's company and wouldn't have it any other way. The kids fight as kids do. But they also snuggle together on the couch to watch the same iPad, or play dress-up for hours or go outside to build a fort.

As a family, we have so much fun exploring new places and trying new things and seeing the joy that everyone experiences. The bonds we are building as a family are fantastic. Both Craig and I are so happy that we get to spend so much quality time together as a family.

There is so much more to see and do.

No matter how long we stay at a place, we always feel like we missed out on doing or seeing something. There are so many cool things out in the world to see and do! Our bucket list goes on and on, so we are happy that we don't have an end date in sight for this adventure, and can just keep adding to our bucket list.

Anything is possible.

As we have pushed our comfort zone and continued with this lifestyle, it has taught us that anything we want to do is possible. It is such a cool feeling when we add an item to our bucket list and know that it isn't just a list of maybes, but a list of things we will really do – it is just a matter of when.

From a personal perspective, we have both seen that our options are limitless if we are willing to put ourselves out there and go for it and be comfortable with a little uncertainty and fear. It really is an amazing feeling!

You only need to shower 1 to 2 times a week.

Seriously, we go 3 to 4 days between showers now, and it is all good. OK, maybe we get a little stinky, but it isn't that bad. It saves so much time when you don't have to take a shower and get ready every day. Just get up, throw on your clothes from yesterday, brush your teeth, put your hair in a ponytail, and you're good to go! If you want to feel a little cleaner, you can always use baby wipes, with or without a few drops of essential oils

Yes, some days it is nice to shower and primp a little, but those days don't happen as often. We aren't looking to impress anyone and usually don't see people we know, so it is all good! We put the funk in RV living with kids!

Our life is about experiences, not things.

Every few months, we go to Goodwill to donate another couple of bags of items. The more time we live with less, the more we want or need less. When we go to the store, we don't want to buy something unless it has a lot of meaning. We aren't looking to fill up our space and time with things.

Instead, we focus on slow living, enjoying our coffee and breakfast in the morning, hanging out by the RV, snuggling in bed. I can't believe the amount of stuff we used to have and the amount of time we put into maintaining and managing it. Living simply is so much more freeing for us, and we want to continue to strive to live an even simpler life.

Yes, the kids still want toys, and yes, we still buy them some. However, they are also good when they are done playing with something. They pass it on to someone else or donate it. By April, they were already donating some of the Christmas presents they had gotten. And when we left friends we'd made in Miami, they gave the kids some of their toys as presents before we left. They just don't attach to many things anymore.

We have ruined ourselves for a normal life.

This is a big one. And to be honest, I have mixed feelings about this. There are still times I miss our old life and our old house. And I feel that by introducing all of us to this lifestyle, it would be tough to go back to our old life. I worry that our kids will continue traveling the world for their whole life. And they'll end up settling down all over the place, and we won't all be in the same location when our kids start having kids. Crazy, right – then why the heck did we do this??

But being a parent is giving our kids the wings and space they need to become who they are. We were willing to take that risk if it meant our kids could have this amazing opportunity to see the world, and that we were able to do it with them before they left the nest and were on their own. We hope that we will always find each other no matter where life takes us, and find ourselves together more often than not through the bond we are building as a family.

Even when things get tough on the road, and I yearn for the stability of a 9 to 5 job, a house, school for the kids, I know I would be bored in a few months and start to get itchy feet again. This life-style is addicting!

No one knows what the future holds and where we will be in 1 year or ten years, but I know for us that this desire for a life outside of the norm isn't going to go away. I am sure it will ebb and flow as the years go on and we all get older, but now that we have awakened this feeling inside ourselves, I don't think it will ever be silenced again!

Two years of RV living with kids. A unique, crazy, scary, fun, exciting, liberating and breathtaking time. An experience that we wouldn't change for anything.

Year 3

It sure has been one crazy adventure, but it has also been unbelievable how much we have learned about each other, our family, and how we want to live our life. We want freedom. Freedom to sleep in, freedom to travel, freedom to set our schedule. Full-time RVing gives us that.

We weren't prepared for that. With freedom comes a lot of choices while living on the road. When you wake up and basically can do what you want with the day, it can be intimidating and confusing. We've consciously chosen to live an unstructured life and love it in many ways. Yet, we also get overwhelmed at times.

What route is right for our family? What would be good for me, for Craig, for our kids?? So many choices as a full-timer!

In some ways, this year has been our biggest year of growth. I think much of that had to do with deciding to become full-time entrepreneurs and no longer being 9-to-5ers. Again, a very empowering feeling, but, it also brings a whole different perspective to things.

After spending two years on the road and traveling with various people and seeing different ways people travel, we understand what this lifestyle is and can be. Plus, our kids are getting older and are transitioning to a new phase in their lives.

To be honest, looking back at when we first hit the road to travel full time, I would have thought three years in, we would know everything about how to travel in an RV and have all the answers figured out. In a lot of ways, I am more confused now than I was back then. However, there are a few things we are pretty clear on and are excited about.

After all that confused rambling, I will see if I can pull this together in bullet points that make more sense.

Things we are clear on as full-time RVers:

We Are Very Clear That Unschooling Is Right For Our Kids

The freedom it gives them is fantastic. Plus, we have seen them "learn" without having set learning times. They have picked up reading without any formal teaching. The kids understand the concept of math without doing any math worksheets. They also know US geography better than I ever did when I was in school. Don't get me wrong, there are still times when we get nervous about going such an unconventional route with our kids, but then we circle right back around to feeling good about it.

We Like Living Simplified

Living in an RV with fewer things to manage and worry about clears up so much space in our heads and so much time in our day. We consistently purge the little we do have to keep it minimal because it feels right. And living in a tiny house is a great way to keep yourself living simply.

It also feels right for the kids. They are happy to donate a toy they know they haven't played with in a while. Yes, they still want to buy and get new things, and we get it for them, but they also see they don't need a whole bunch of things.

It really is a freeing feeling and is addictive, and you want to learn how to live with less and less! I love that the RV lifestyle and living in a small rig without much storage space has helped us make this a priority, and continues to push us to evaluate everything we do and purchase.

We Like Being Weird

I got asked the other day if it would bother me to be judged about our choices. I could confidently and clearly say that I don't care if someone else judges me for my choices.

We are making conscious choices that are not dictated by a work schedule or school schedule. They are not dictated by trying to fit in or keep up with the Joneses.

Are they the right choices for every family out there? No, and that is OK. To each his own. Do your own thing and be proud of that.

We don't live our life the way other people or society think we should. We live our life the way we want to.

Above all, this is something we are very proud of and sure about. With the freedom lifestyle we have created, we aren't in situations where we have to be concerned about what we look like or if we are all squeaky clean each day. Another of the many benefits if you live and travel full-time in your RV.

We have met families who have commented on how much time goes into making sure their kids' fingernails are clean and their clothes are spotless before sending them to school. That's not something we have to worry about. People expect others (especially kids) to have a little dirt under their nails and on their clothes at a campground.

Being Entrepreneurs Is Empowering

I didn't grow up thinking I would be an entrepreneur, and it wasn't a goal of mine until it was. Now that we have gone down this path, it is empowering to see that we can make our own money. And that we can set our schedule, sleep in on a Monday and work on a Sunday or really whenever we want to. The freedom is stressful but also exciting!

Part of living as entrepreneurs means we have to be OK with a level of worry and stress around making sure we are bringing enough money in. There are no paid vacations or sick days. It has been an adjustment and something we continue to learn how to live with, but it is also really cool and makes us proud that we live our own lives and set our own schedule.

We Like Sharing Our Story To Encourage Others To Live Their Dream

Almost everyone that decides to travel full time thinks about starting a travel blog at some point. I mean, it is perfect. We are out seeing all of these places, so, of course, we should blog about it and share it with people!

I didn't anticipate the community we would build and the amazing supporters and followers we would have on this journey. It is so cool to have a group of people who follow our journey, encourage us and provide their insight.

Having a community and hearing from them makes us want to provide them with more. We enjoy inspiring people to live their dreams, showing what we have been through and what we are going through, and providing an example of a different lifestyle to live with kids.

Where To Stay

After being on a three-year road trip, we have learned that we like campgrounds sometimes – a nice pool and a nice cement pad can be a good break for a few days. But we also really like the National Park and State Park campgrounds which have a more relaxed vibe.

We have been getting more into boondocking on free land and would like to continue to do that.

We know that we are not people who want to jump from campground to campground, but instead want some variety. This also includes mixing in hotel and house stays when we can.

Comfort Zones

Comfort zones are made for pushing, and ours keeps getting larger and larger. My sister had mentioned this when we first started, and it has continued to hold true. Once you push your comfort zone a little, it keeps stretching and stretching. I am amazed every day at how far ours has stretched.

It is another aspect of this life that is so freeing. Knowing we can do more than we ever thought was possible is inspiring and fuels us to keep pushing it. We have left what some would say is the "real world" behind and created our version of what we want OUR real world to look like.

There Is Always Something More

This is a challenge. Part of the reason we have been able to do so many amazing things is that we are always pushing and looking. But part of the challenge is that it is hard to take a step back and enjoy what we have accomplished to date.

I would say this year is all about trying to be more present, slowing down and appreciating everything we have accomplished and done to date. But, that's easier said than done!

We Are Still Scared

I would think that after three years of full-time living on the road, all of our fears about this lifestyle would be gone. Nope . . . they are still there. Things like safety in an RV park, weather (I HATE storms in the RV), going somewhere new and not knowing what to expect, and should we have a home base?

We almost didn't go to Canada this year because we were so worried about the unknown.

We are planning to head to Mexico in January, and we still get this fearful feeling in the pit of our stomach. But we have learned we can do so much even when scared. We just can't let fear stand in our way.

I don't think the fear will ever go away, but our ability to manage it has gotten so much better.

Marriage Is Hard And Takes Work

This transition to full-time entrepreneurs has pushed Craig and me to dive deeper into our relationship and how we work together. We will be the first to tell you we do not work the same. I like to go at 110 miles an hour and dive into everything and push through it. Craig wants to take a slower approach where he analyzes things and doesn't like to have too many things going on at one time. Yes, that is a formula for arguments and disaster. Not to mention, we live in less than 200 square feet of space.

Ashley from the "Mama Says Namaste" blog had some great personality profiles that helped Craig and I learn more about each other. Plus, we did the free Love Languages test, and it opened our eyes to how we can work together as a couple, parents and business partners.

We haven't found all the answers. But every argument or fight we get into, has helped us grow closer and improve our relationship. It is still a work in progress, and I think it will always be that way.

But it is worth it to both of us to keep working at it. And to keep our relationship as epic and amazing as we know it can be!

We Still Don't Really Know What We Are Doing.

Our oldest turned ten this year. 10 – that is double digits! We have a ten-year-old, yet we still don't feel like we know what we are doing as parents. Do you ever?!

His reaching this age has made me stop and think how crazy fast life is. And how we can't spend all this time trying to do it perfectly and right, but instead have to sit back and just enjoy it sometimes. As we go along this journey, we're continually figuring things out, but the more we learn, the more we see how much we don't know.

This brings me back to what this year will be about. Being present in the current moment, taking time to smell the roses, and genuinely enjoying this amazing life we have!

After year 3, I didn't write these posts anymore. Now I wish I would have! Actually, though, all of this still holds true in so many ways. This lifestyle provides so much opportunity for personal growth and family growth. Why move into an RV and continue to live the way you always have? Instead, use this time to expand, learn and change your perspective on things.

Up next is the last chapter in the book. Thanks for staying around this long! I hope you have gotten a lot of useful insights and tips about full-time RVing with kids. The last chapter talks about the biggest thing that stops people from hitting the road . . .

Chapter 26

The #1 Thing That Stops People

The #1 thing that stops people from living their dreams is FEAR. It almost prevented us from starting our Crazy Family Adventure. Several times.

Where Does Fear Come From?

Fear stems from so many places, which is why it is so hard to manage and overcome. Here are a few examples of our fears:

- Not having enough money
- Not knowing how to do something
- The unknown
- Not knowing if you are capable enough
- What people will think of you
- Not being normal
- Ruining our kid's lives

These fears, and many more, hold people back from taking steps to start living their dream lives. I will tell you right now, we were scared out of our minds throughout the whole process of selling our house, moving into an RV and then starting our own business.

And I will let you in on a little secret. We are STILL scared out of our minds. We are starting to realize it isn't about not being scared; it is about not letting that fear hold us back from tackling the things we want to do.

Yes, life would be more comfortable if we never faced any fears. But that would also mean we would be living in fear of fear. We choose not to do that. Instead, we want to push our comfort zones and see where that can take us.

This is not an easy process for us, and there have been lots of fights, arguments, tears and disagreements. But each of those times helped us grow as people and learn how to manage our fears.

I would be lying if I said I thought we were ever going to get past the fear. As parents, fear is a constant that never goes away. As a business owner, it is always there. Yes, we can get better at ignoring it or learning how to cope with it. But it will always be there. Lurking.

Our goal is to learn how to handle that fear and turn it into a positive emotion. We don't want fear to stop us from experiencing amazing things. And we don't want our kids to grow up thinking they have to be afraid of the unknown.

Being an entrepreneur and having our own business has opened a whole other avenue of fear for us. We are 9 to 5ers. Both Craig or I had always had a 9 to 5 job with a consistent paycheck and benefits. Becoming business owners has been SCARY!

And I don't see that stopping any time soon. Instead, we know if we face our fears, there are so many great opportunities out there. If we lived in fear of fear day in and day out, we would miss out on so much.

I think part of dealing with this fear is accepting we may not always be happy with the outcome, but we understand that going through the journey is all part of the process. Each fear we face teaches us more about ourselves and our relationship with each other and with our kids.

Now, when fear starts to creep in, I take a deep breath and say STOP! I will not let fear determine my life, but will continue to push through it. We have also found amazing things happen on the other side of fear. You just have to be willing to move past it.

Your ducks will never all be in a row, things will never be perfect, there will always be something to worry about. But if you want to try this lifestyle, just do it. You will figure it out as you go. Or you may figure out it isn't for you. But at least you tried!

I am going to end the book with one of my favorite quotes:

"Twenty years from now, you will be more disappointed by the things that you didn't do than by the ones you did do. So throw off the bowlines. Sail away from the safe harbor. Catch the trade winds in your sails. Explore. Dream. Discover." Mark Twain

Live Q & A Session

If you are interested in one of our live question and answer sessions on full-time RVing with kids, you can learn more here:

www.crazyfamilyadventure.com/CFAQandA

(There is also a free gift: Our 15 Favorite RV Spots Guide!)

If you are interested in learning more about Crazy Family Adventure and additional things we offer. Checkout:

Newsletter: www.crazyfamilyadventure.com/newsletter

Podcast: https://www.crazyfamilyadventure.com/cfa-podcast/

Blog: www.crazyfamilyadventure.com

YouTube: https://www.youtube.com/c/crazyfamilyadventure

Instagram: https://www.instagram.com/crazyfamilyadventure

Facebook: https://www.facebook.com/crazyfamilyadventure

Pinterest: https://www.pinterest.com/crazyfamilyadve/

www.ingramcontent.com/pod-product-compliance
Lightning Source LLC
Chambersburg PA
CBHW071600150726
48000CB00004B/1538